Samsung
SmartTV Application
Development:
A Complete Guide

Samsung
SmartTV®
Application Development

Handstudio Co., Ltd

Forewords by Hyogun Lee, R&D Office Leader,
Senior Vice President of Visual Display Division, Samsung Electronics
& Joonhee Ahn, Handstudio CEO

WILEY

I want to first take this opportunity to thank you for reading *Samsung SmartTV Application Development*. You have made a wise decision, both in the platform you've chosen and the book you are holding. This guide comes straight from the team that built the world's leading smart TV—the Samsung SmartTV—a platform that is new and bursting with potential.

The historical impact of TV is undeniable. Television has been the dominant media force in much of the world for over half a century. The events that we have collectively experienced thanks to TV—triumph and tragedy, news and entertainment, drama and reality—have been the source of the defining images of our time.

But it's not just what we watch, it's how we watch that has also shaped our world. Since its introduction, the TV became the focal point of many households and a natural place for families and friends to gather around. In the broadcast era, popular programs could drive so-called "appointment viewing," with viewers planning their schedules around their favorite TV programs. Later technologies like VCRs, DVRs, and Video on Demand then provided some degree of flexibility—and marked the beginning of the watch "what you want, when you want it" era.

Now we are well into the Internet era, with a level of freedom, personalization, and convenience that was once only dreamed about. High bandwidth connections allow customers to stream content to their PCs and smart phones. Among all this new technology, consumers have found themselves asking, "Why can't my TV do this?" SmartTV provides an answer: "It can."

As a TV application developer, you can enable the freedom that audiences desire from their TVs. You can bring them the content, the entertainment, and the interaction that they are expecting. Or perhaps you'll choose to create innovative experiences by leveraging SmartTV features in new and unexpected ways.

No device is an island, and the Samsung SmartTV has been designed to be a vital part of the consumer's complete entertainment ecosystem. With convergence technologies that connect SmartTV with PCs, tablets, and smart phones, app developers are now exposed to a new world of opportunities. For example, the Samsung SmartTV Smart Interaction feature allows for voice and gesture input, providing endless possibilities for new games, apps, and experiences.

I hope that reading this book gives you the power to turn your ideas into reality. Platforms succeed because of developer support. In this "Age of the App," consumers expect a rich and diverse set of applications for their products—and developer support is key for meeting that expectation. I am proud and honored that you have chosen to develop for Samsung SmartTV, and we will continue to work to earn your confidence.

What is the next killer app for SmartTV? How high will our imaginations go? That is for you to decide. This book is just a guide. You are the pilot.

Suwon, South Korea – July 2013
Hyogun Lee, R&D Office Leader, Senior Vice President of Visual Display Business,
Samsung Electronics

IT innovation that has created the "smart" phone is now expanding the innovation to TV—the true king of home electronics. The new SmartTV moved beyond receiving broadcasted service into contents services such as video game, education, sports, and video-on-demand. As smart phone applications did, SmartTV applications are also creating a new apps store based on an open ecosystem that directly connects providers with consumers. However, this emerging market has not been fully accessible to contents providers because there has been a lack of application development tools and know-how for new developers.

Handstudio has led the SmartTV application development for the past four years, since the inception of the technology, and is willing to share all its knowledge and know-how with the new developers through this book.

The Samsung SmartTV has led the world's SmartTV market and continuously reinvented the technology into the new 2013 standard—irresistible to anyone who comes to notice it. Gesture and motion recognition features have become refined and stabilized in the last year, and enabled developers to create unique features not available on other platforms. The Samsung SmartTV's standard-adhering web-based application development environment allows easier transition to web developers, which is why Handstudio picked the Samsung SmartTV to introduce its SmartTV app development method.

Handstudio and all its members have been preaching for the SmartTV platform's possibility and market prospect for the last four years. The year 2013 is now the exploding moment of SmartTV's new innovations and popularity. It is also the best and the most emotional moment for us to finally publish this book. This book is dedicated to all who encouraged us, and especially to those who guided us and wrote recommendations for the book. Thank you.

Dear developers, here is the wonderful new platform awaiting new heroes. With this book, take the chance and become the master of the promising new SmartTV platform.

Lastly, I sincerely thank Vice President Kwangkee Lee, Principal Engineer Kiho Kim, and Principal Engineer Taedong Lee at Samsung Electronics for their efforts in publishing this book.

Thank you.

Joonhee Ahn, Handstudio CEO

Table of Contents

13 Advanced Features

14 Exception Handling

15 From the SDF to the App Store

Addendum Hands Frame Source Code

01

Introducing the Samsung SmartTV Platform

Introducing SmartTV

What Is a SmartTV?

As an adjective the word "smart" is used to describe a new device capable of more advanced functions. For example, a smart phone supports not only basic Internet access, but also PC-level information processing and high-definition multimedia playback, transcending from a traditional cellular phone into a new device that can substitute most of the PC functions. As the information processing power transmuted a cellular phone into a smart phone, a SmartTV was also created by adding computing power to a TV. A user can use various additional contents such as movies, video games, searches, and other fused or smart services, with a highly accessible UI/UX environment, provided by a digital TV's operating system.

As a smart phone has an operating system such as Google's Android or Apple's iOS, a SmartTV comes with its own operating system. You will see that a Samsung SmartTV uses the WebKit browser on Linux as its base operating system, which harmonizes multi-tiered elements to provide vital functions to operate a SmartTV.

Figure 1-1. The Samsung SmartTV 2013's Smart Hub

Another characteristic of a SmartTV is a standard application hub. Just as a smart phone platform has an app store, a SmartTV platform has an app store with a developer ecosystem. SmartTV app stores are already servicing thousands of applications categorized into movies, games, sports, lifestyle, information, education, etc. Note that a SmartTV app's special UI/UX, which utilizes TV's unique properties such as a large screen, is capturing consumers with a new appeal.

Evolving into a smart device does not change a device's basic purpose, and a TV's basic purpose is consuming broadcasted contents. New functions of a SmartTV must not get in the way of watching TV broadcasting. Samsung SmartTV provides various VOD applications to support the basic purpose. Applications that help obtain related information during a broadcasted program are also well received.

The Samsung SmartTV, as the leader in the TV industry, has introduced new smart functions such as Smart Evolution, Smart Interaction, and Smart Recommendation to redefine the standard of a SmartTV year after year, in addition to advancements for the basic TV function of watching broadcasted programs, such as high screen quality.

Many manufacturers have also joined the SmartTV market. Competition among them has been rapidly expanding the SmartTV market, just as competition has expanded the smart phone market. As the SmartTV evolves, the application ecosystem grows as well. Developers are facing an era of new opportunities that the SmartTV brings.

History of the Samsung SmartTV

The Connected TV introduced basic Internet capability to a TV, and even utilized the new Web 2.0 trend and provided RSS-based Internet information. The Connected TV later became the Internet TV, which introduced an application service platform. Unlike the current Samsung SmartTV, the Internet TV application was in Java Widget style. As the application market grew, Samsung Electronics published an SDK (Software Development Kit) for developers.

Figure 1-2. History of Samsung's TV Technology

Samsung introduced the currently serving application hub, Samsung Apps, in 2010 for the first time. This enabled consumers to purchase apps on the application hub and use them on their TV sets.

In 2011, the application hub had evolved into a smart hub with newly introduced Internet TV function and multimedia content. Web browser performance was also improved and provided a perfect environment for SmartTV applications to thrive. The SDF (Samsung Developer's Forum) was launched to provide app support to developers with all skill levels.

In 2012, Samsung SmartTV added the AllShare function that supports content sharing between Samsung devices, and the application market started to expand in both quality and quantity as indicated by the increased content on Samsung Apps.

Samsung SmartTV continued to revolutionize in 2013. Newly added smart functions include Smart Interaction, which supports gesture and voice recognition, and personalized content recommendations. Improved hardware enhances animation performance. Samsung also expanded functions selection, which resulted in enhanced applications with a faster response time.

Samsung SmartTV Specifications

Samsung SmartTV has the following standard specifications

Feature	Description
OS	Linux 2.6
Screen Resolution	• Application: 1280 x 720, 960 x 540, 32 bpp • Smart Hub: 1280 x 720, 32 bpp • VOD: 1920 x 1080, 32 bpp

Table 1-1. Samsung SmartTV Standard Specifications

The following table compares hardware specification and supported functions of the corresponding SDK version in 2012 and 2013. Player specification is not included here because it will be explained in chapter 7 in detail.

Component	Feature	2012		2013	
		TV/AV	SDK 3.0	TV/AV	SDK 4.5
App Engine	HTML	HTML5	HTML5	HTML5	HTML5
	DOM	DOM3	DOM3	DOM3	DOM3
	CSS	CSS3	CSS3	CSS3	CSS3
	JavaScript	SquirrelFish	SquirrelFish	SquirrelFish	V8
Flash	Browser Plug-in	SWF	Flash 10.1, ActionScript 3.0	Flash 10.1, ActionScript 3.0	Flash 11.1, ActionScript 3.0	Flash 11.1, ActionScript 3.0
	Stand-alone	SWF	Flash 10.1, ActionScript 3.0	Flash 10.1, ActionScript 3.0	Flash 11.1, ActionScript 3.0	Flash 11.1, ActionScript 3.0
Flash	AIR	AIR	AR (2012): (TV D6000 or higher, Blu-ray player D6700 or higher)	Not Supported	AR (2012): (TV D6000 or higher, Blu-ray player D6700 or higher)	AIR 3.0
	Streaming	Streaming	RTMP, RTMPe	RTMP, RTMPe	RTMP, RTMPe	RTMP, RTMPe

Component	Feature	2012		2013	
		TV/AV	SDK 3.0	TV/AV	SDK 4.5
DRM	WMDRM 10 PD	PlayReady	Not Supported	PlayReady	Not Supported
	PlayReady	Supported	Not Supported	Supported	Not Supported
	Widevine	Supported	Not Supported	Supported	Not Supported

Table 1-2. Specifications for Samsung SmartTV 2012 and 2013

The current standard is Samsung SmartTV 2013 with a SDK version of 4.x.

Note that this book will cover all areas of application development based on Samsung SmartTV 2012 and 2013 models.

Samsung SmartTV SDK

Structure of the Samsung SmartTV SDK

Samsung SmartTV SDK can be downloaded from the official SDF (Samsung Developers Forum) and provides several tools for application development. See the following table for minimum system requirements for using the SDK.

Hardware Requirements

CPU	Dual-core, 1.5 GHz or single-core 3 GHz or higher
Memory	2GB or more
OS	Windows 7 (Recommended), Windows XP Service Pack 2 or higher Mac OS X: Intel-based hardware, 10.6 and above Linux: All versions that support Virtual Box 2.4.2
Screen Resolution	1280 x 1024 or higher
HDD	5GB or more

Table 1-3. Hardware Requirements for Samsung SmartTV Application Development

Software Requirements

For All Operating Systems
- Java SE 1.6 or higher

For Windows
- .NET Framework 2.0
- Latest version of Visual C++ 2005 Redistributable Package and Visual C++ 2010 Redistributable Package
- DirectX End-User Runtime

Notice in the hardware requirements that Linux and Mac OS are supported since the last update of Samsung SmartTV SDK 4.0, to support a multi-platform development environment. Although not all Windows SDK functions are supported by Linux and Mac OS versions, they are more than suitable for basic application development.

This demonstrates Samsung's enthusiasm to support Samsung SmartTV application ecosystem and developers.

▶ Note : http://www.samsungdforum.com/Devtools/SdkReleaseNote

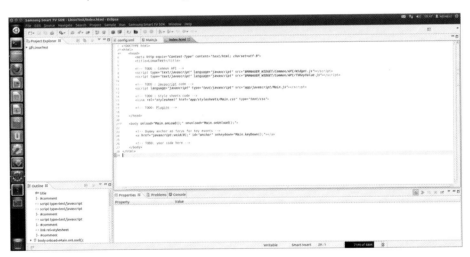

Figure 1-3. Samsung SmartTV SDK for Linux

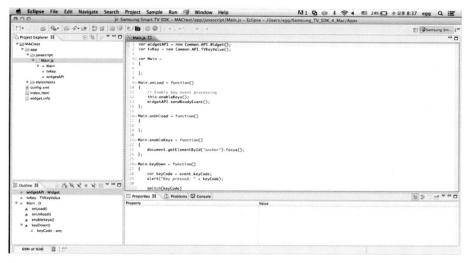

Figure 1-4. Samsung SmartTV SDK for Mac OS X

Samsung SmartTV SDK consists of an application IDE (Integrated Development Environment), SmartTV Emulators to test developed applications, and the Apache web server to package and distribute the SDK.

The SmartTV IDE

From version 4.x, Samsung SmartTV's IDE was changed to a plug-in for the Eclipse IDE, instead of using its own edit tool. The IDE provides optimized project development and management tools, including a text editor for SmartTV applications.

The SmartTV Emulators

The SDK includes SmartTV Emulators for each platform version so that application developers can test their applications without having SmartTV sets.

SDK 4.5 includes a VirtualBox-based emulator that supports Samsung SmartTV 2013 models only. Use SDK 4.0's emulator for previous models.

Each emulator has a basic controller and a smart type virtual remote controller, console window interface, and the Web Inspector debugging tool. The console window allows monitoring execution information with preset JavaScript logs.

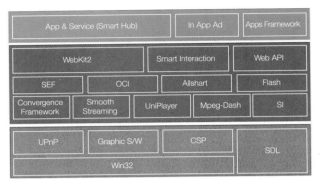

Figure 1-5. Structure of SmartTV Emulator Software

The Apache web server

The Apache web server is necessary to run the SDK and is provided during the SDK installation. Or you can use an already installed or different version and modify the SDK's web server directory option.

Samsung SmartTV's SDK Support

Samsung Electronics has provided the SDK since 2009 to support TV developers. See below for the SDK's version history.

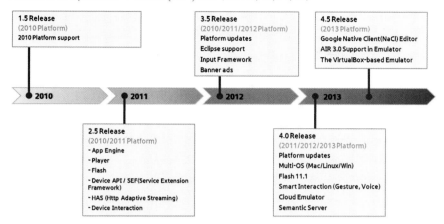

The SDK is updated 4 times per year (BETA, .0, .1, .5)

Figure 1-6. Samsung SDK Version History

The SDK was upgraded to 4.x versions during 2013. The new version has the following major improvements.

- WYSIWYG style code editor
- Smart Interaction: new gestures for added movement senses
- App Framework: 2013 app engine (HTML5 – Video/Audio, WebSocket, WebGL)
- UniPlayer
- SEF
- Convergence Framework
- OCI (Open Convergence Interface): MIDI support
- AllShare
- In-app ads
- Flash 11.1
- Smooth Streaming
- Web Inspector
- ATT (automated test tool): testing tool for event log/play
- NaCl

Notably, the new version has a WYSIWYG editor to conveniently develop a UI component; new Smart Interaction gestures, including the Swipe gesture and the Thumbs-up gesture; reinforced convergence support through the Convergence Framework; and the Web Inspector debugger/ATT to support testing.

Google Native Client (NaCl)

The Google Native Client (NaCl) is an open-source project that allows native code to be executed safely in a web browser. This powerful feature lets developers write C/C++ applications that can run at near native speeds in a web application. More programming languages will be supported by NaCl in the future.

NaCl provides many benefits for application developers. Existing C/C++ applications can be migrated to the web much more easily by using NaCl. Additionally, performance is significantly increased as applications can run at speeds comparable to desktop applications. 2D/3D graphics, audio, and input events can all be supported without requiring additional plugins.

NaCl executables are built for a specific target architecture such as ARM or x86. To make NaCl technology more portable, Portable NaCl (PNaCl) was introduced. The PNaCl executable is designed to be hardware independent. At the moment, though, PNaCl applications cannot be run directly. They must be converted back to a NaCl executable. The current approach for platform independence is to distribute PNaCl executables that can be translated on the host machine into the appropriate NaCl format.

The Pepper Plug-in API (PPAPI) allows communication between NaCl apps and web applications. For example, NaCl applications can exchange data with the JavaScript code of a web application. Additionally, the NaCl application can use the Pepper interfaces to use browser resources.

The SmartTV and SDK support PNaCl applications. Developers can code and compile a PNaCl application in the SmartTV IDE. Additionally, they can run the application in the SmartTV Emulator. A SmartTV PNaCl application consists of several sets of files:

- HTML, CSS, and JavaScript files: These files make the basic structure of any SmartTV application.

- Native Client module: The compiled native executable. Multiple native executables can be included to support various hardware architectures.

- NaCl manifest: Specifies which native executable should be used for a particular architecture.

- SmartTV SDK configuration files: Specify the properties of the SmartTV application.

In the SmartTV SDK IDE, the developer can choose to create a stand-alone C/C++ PNaCl module, or to wrap it in a SmartTV web application. The IDE provides options to test the application in the Chrome browser or the SmartTV Emulator.

SDF

Introducing the SDF

The SDF is a website that provides everything necessary for Samsung SmartTV application development, from downloading the SDK to uploading finished applications. Let's briefly review its main menu.

Figure 1-7. The SDF's Main Menu

The SDF's Main Menu

- **News & Event:** Announces new Samsung SmartTV SDK versions, site reorganization, and system maintenance schedules.

- **SDK:** Provides SDK download page for developers. This page provides version history for the Samsung SmartTV SDK and release notes to summarize additional functions for each version.

- **Guide:** This is the official API documentation. It has all application development references, with examples and tutorials for each function. The guide has a well-designed index and search functions for easy access to necessary information.

- **Forum:** Separate forms for English, Korean, Chinese, and Russian languages are provided for Samsung SmartTV application developers to share their knowledge. Practical tips not available in the Guide are often discussed. Also Samsung's engineers are actively participating to promote the forum activities, and help developers in debugging and providing technical solutions.

- **Support:** The Support page provides FAQ and Samsung SmartTV application policy, such as UI/UX and security guidelines.

- **My Work:** Developers can register and distribute their own applications on the app store from this site. Samsung's application auditing process for quality assurance can be monitored here. Developers can also use this site to maintain and upgrade published applications.

Summary

Samsung Electronics has launched SmartTV products since 2010, and created an application hub that goes beyond a TV's traditional broadcast receiving function to create a new market for application contents. Developers are facing new business opportunities in the new content market growing with the SmartTV. Samsung Electronics is actively supporting the TV application development ecosystem with the Samsung SmartTV SDK. SmartTV is becoming the core of all smart devices, led by the revolutionizing Samsung SmartTV.

02

App Development on Samsung SmartTV

Structure of a Samsung SmartTV Application

Structure of a Samsung SmartTV Application

A Samsung SmartTV application runs on the WebKit browser engine. This means that a SmartTV application is similar to a common website based on HTML pages. However, a SmartTV application has a distinct difference from a common website; unlike a website with variable resolution and keyboard and mouse input, a SmartTV application runs on fixed resolution with remote controller input. SmartTV users are already accustomed to navigating with a remote controller's directional, Enter, and Back keys.

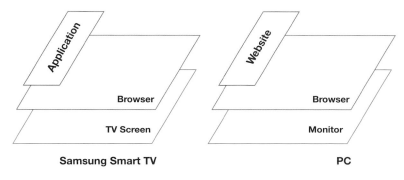

Figure 2-1. Structure of a Samsung SmartTV Application

The above figure demonstrates the structural difference of a website and a TV application. From 2012, Samsung SmartTV has been using the standard WebKit browser engine that is also used by Google Chrome and Apple Safari, instead of its previous MAPLE (Markup Engine Platform for Embedded System) application engine.

For all practical purposes, the Samsung SmartTV application is similar to front-end development of a common web service. Business logic such as server calls and event handling are implemented with JavaScript, and graphical interfaces are designed with CSS and HTML pages.

Application Resolution

A SmartTV application supports HD-level 1280 x 720 and 960 x 540 resolutions. The majority of applications for 2013 TVs are designed with 1280 x 720 resolution. Also, high-end 2012 and 2013 models support full HD (1920 x 1080) resolution.

Application Types

Samsung SmartTV applications can be categorized into the following types, based on how they are displayed on screen.

Application Type	Description	Screen Layout
Full-Screen Application	Displayed using an entire TV screen.	
Single-Wide Application	Displayed using part of a TV screen. This type can run while the viewer is watching a TV program.	
Ticker	Also displayed using part of a TV screen and can run while the viewer is watching a TV program, but it's smaller than a single-wide application.	

Table 2-1. Application Types

As shown above, there are full-screen applications, single-wide applications that occupy some screen area, and ticker applications that float on a screen.

Project Types

One of the following three project types needs to be selected while you're creating a new Samsung SmartTV application project. Each project type has the following characteristics:

- Basic App Project: Uses a WYSIWYG visual code editor for easy application development.
- Flash App Project: Implemented in Adobe Flash. Samsung SmartTV supports Flash-based applications with a selection of Flash functions and components suitable for TV applications.
- JavaScript App Project: The most common project that can utilize the most of the Samsung SmartTV platform's capability. It can even control the lifecycle and processes of an application.

  ※ This book covers the last JavaScript App Project type.

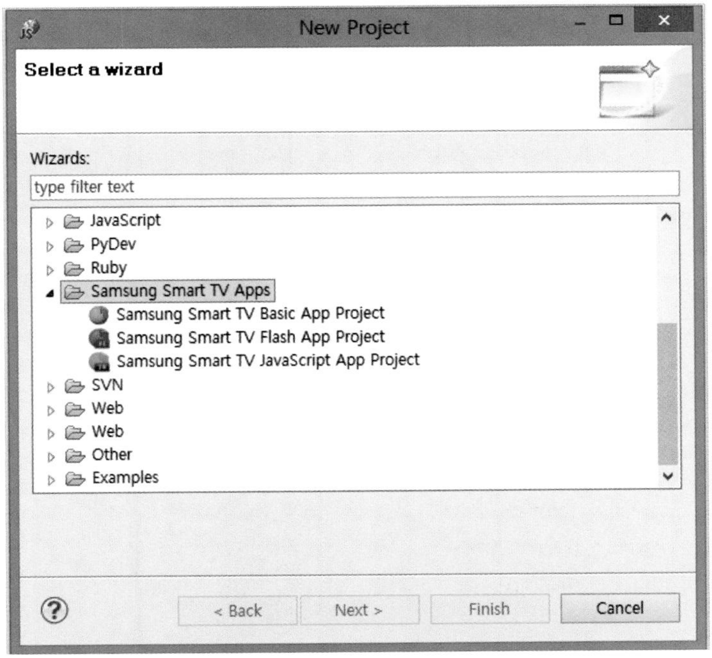

Figure 2-2. Available Project Types

Basic App Project

The Basic App Project type is useful for beginners because it provides a visual editing tool not supported by other project types. It can utilize various Samsung UI components on a WYSIWYG editor to easily design an application layout.

The WYSIWYG editor can add, edit, or delete UI components using an XML file. The XML file has the .scene extension, and is grouped with automatically created HTML, CSS, and JavaScript files with the same name. The created files and the XML file consist of a scene, which functions as a display screen layer of a SmartTV application.

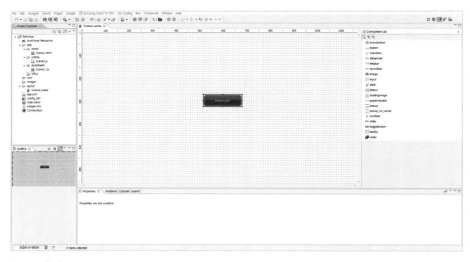

Figure 2-3. A Basic App Project

Figure 2-4. The WYSIWYG Editor's UI Component Library

As shown on the right, a project's layout is first designed in the WYSIWYG editor. Then the saved project file can be clicked with the right mouse button to choose the "Sync with Code" function to automatically create HTML, CSS, and JavaScript files for the project.

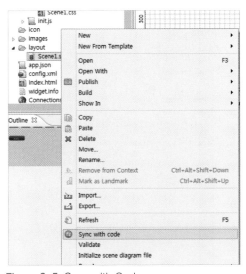

Figure 2-5. Sync with Code

(Visit http://www.samsungdforum.com/ Guide/d04/main_features/synchronize.html for examples.)

The Basic App project's UI components are designed in Samsung SmartTV's basic UI style. Knowledge in components structure and manual CSS code editing is necessary to modify the design.

Flash App Project

A Flash App Project utilizes internal Flash support of a Samsung SmartTV. Adobe Flash Professional version software is required in addition to the Samsung SmartTV SDK. Source code is programmed in the Flash software, and the SDK is used to test and package the application. A Flash App Project also uses standard JavaScript API by including the Flash object in the index.html file.

Unlike other project types, the Flash File ID and Path need to be configured while creating a Flash App Project.

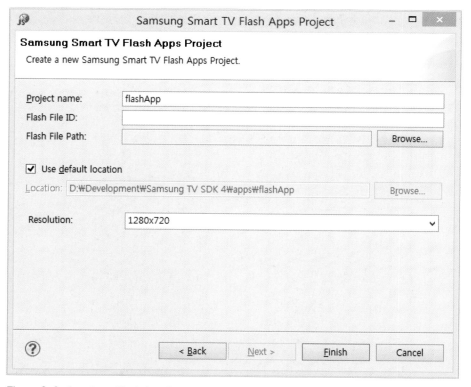

Figure 2-6. Creating a Flash App Project

Please note that a SmartTV has a limited Flash player that cannot match performance of an emulator running on a PC. For example, a SmartTV can only process 30 frames per second for a Flash animation. Please keep this performance limitation of a SmartTV in mind while designing a Flash App Project.

Figure 2-7. Structure of a Flash App Project

JavaScript App Project

As briefly mentioned, the JavaScript App Project is the standard SmartTV development method and is the focus of this book. Because the majority of standard device APIs and application lifecycle processes are implemented in JavaScript, this project type allows a developer fine control of native APIs.

JavaScript app programming is also easy to learn for a developer experienced in web application, because it uses the same standard web development method.

This is the most versatile project type because it allows developers to go beyond Samsung's SDF guidelines and to directly access all application components.

Figure 2-8. Structure of a JavaScript App Project

Web Application

As shown previously, a Samsung SmartTV application is implemented as a web application. While this does not support all web technologies including server side containers or server side programming languages, a Samsung SmartTV application has almost a similar front-end structure that allows using custom web client development practices.

This also means it is critical to understand general web environments and HTML (its building blocks); CSS (its style maker); and JavaScript (its binding agent).

HTML in SmartTV Programming

There are different HTML file structures to accommodate scene design, which is a page or a screen layer design of a SmartTV application. This book will introduce a scene-based programming technique that uses layers, instead of separate HTML files, to handle each scene. Therefore, only one top-level HTML file—index.html—will be used. Screens contained in HTML layers, anchors to handle focuses, and objects with necessary device APIs are all included in the index.html file. As in a website, the HTML file represents the application itself as its starting point.

CSS in SmartTV Programming

CSS defines display styles. It is even more vital to handle design elements with CSS on an application that runs on a SmartTV with limited processing power and screen resolution.

JavaScript in SmartTV Programming

JavaScript is the execution code that runs the application. It calls device APIs, handles DOM elements for events, and manages focus and scene transactions for a SmartTV application. All necessary functions and event handling can be implemented using JavaScript.

Summary

Samsung SmartTV application development is similar to common website development because it also runs on a browser. Pay attention to application specifications such as screen resolution, and it will be a breeze for any web programmer to develop an application. SmartTV application development supports the following three project types.

- WYSIWYG-based Basic App Projects that utilize standard Samsung UI components
- Flash-based Flash App projects
- JavaScript App Projects implemented purely with JavaScript

03

Preparations for App Development

Chapter 3 will demonstrate downloading the Samsung SmartTV SDK and configuring an actual development environment on a Windows-based system.

SDK Download and Installation

Previewing the SDF

As mentioned previously, the Samsung SmartTV SDK can be downloaded and installed from the Samsung Developers Forum (http://www.samsungdforum.com). Select the SDK menu from the site's top-most menu bar to open the next page.

Figure 3-1. The SDK Page on the SDF

Select the SDK menu's submenu, the "SDK Download," to open the download page for the SDK.

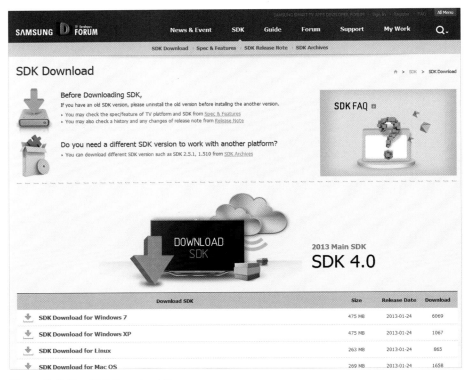

Figure 3-2. The SDK Download Page

The SDK Download page provides the latest SDK 4.5 version, as well as previous versions, for Windows and other operating systems. It also provides system requirements on hardware and software for SmartTV application development, and release notes.

The SDF had supported only the Windows operating system in the past, but started also supporting Linux and Mac since SDK version 4.0. However, it is still better to use the Windows version since the Linux and Mac versions have limitations on functions and APIs.

The SDF also provides an Emulator image for Oracle VirtualBox to support running the Emulator on Linux and Mac operating systems, and a local cloud development environment to support collaboration of developers using multiple platforms.

SDK Download and Installation

Chapters 1 and 2 defined the development environment used in this book. As such, only Windows examples for SDK downloading and installing the SDK will be discussed, and Linux and Mac operating systems will not be covered.

Click the "SDK Download for Windows 7" link as shown on Figure 3-3 to download the SDK.

Download SDK	Size	Release Date	Download
SDK Download for Windows 7	475 MB	2013-01-24	2619
SDK Download for Windows XP	475 MB	2013-01-24	483
SDK Download for Linux	263 MB	2013-01-24	387
SDK Download for Mac OS	269 MB	2013-01-24	778
SDK Emulator Image for Virtual Box	728 MB	2013-01-04	1938
Local Cloud Development Environment	1641 MB	2013-01-04	565
Semantic Server 32bit	44 MB	2013-01-04	403

Figure 3-3. Downloading the SDK

The SDK download is a large file size because it includes an IDE. Please make sure that there is enough available hard drive space. Execute the downloaded installation file to open the installation window as shown in Figure 3-4.

Figure 3-4. SDK Installation Step 1

Click the "Next" button to proceed to the next screen on Figure 3-5, selecting components for the Editor, which is an IDE, and the Emulator. Select all components for now and continue the installation.

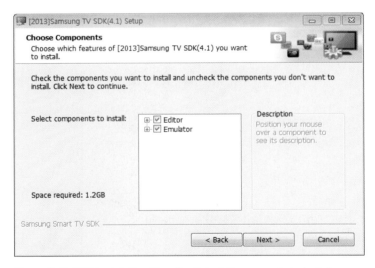

Figure 3-5. SDK Installation Step 2 – Select Components to Install

Next, choose the installation folder and continue the installation.

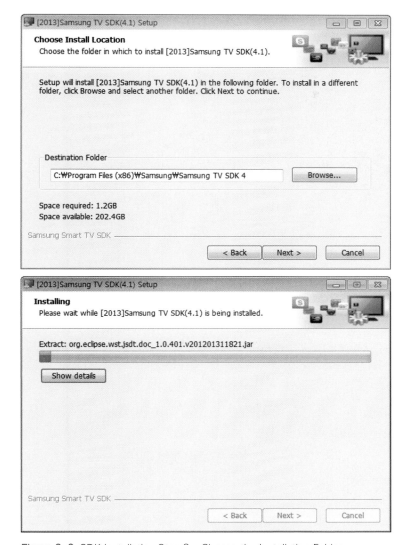

Figure 3-6. SDK Installation Step 3 – Choose the Installation Folder

After the SDK installation is complete, continue to the Apache web server installation, which acts as the local web server for applications to be tested. You may skip this step if an Apache web server is already installed on the PC.

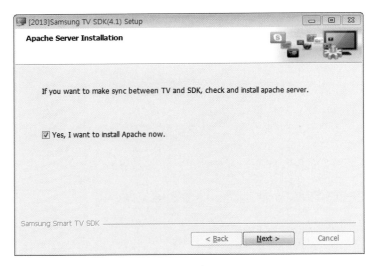

Figure 3-7. Installing the Apache Web Server

The installed SDK can be accessed on the Windows Start menu or directly in the "Samsung TV SDK 4" subfolder of the installation folder entered in Step 3. Also, look below for the shortcut icon created on the Windows Desktop.

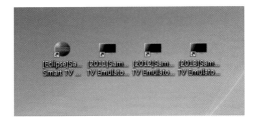

Figure 3-8. SDK Desktop Shortcut

Configuration

There are a few additional configuration steps for a smoother development environment.

Configuring the Project Workspace

The default Eclipse workspace is "C:\Users\Administrator\workspace."

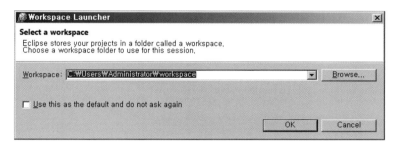

Figure 3-9. Configuring the Eclipse Workspace

For the fast execution of an application on the Emulator, enter "SDK Installation Folder app" as the workspace. This enables an Emulator to only check project folders on the Windows file system and quickly run without the delayed loading time associated with Eclipse.

Eclipse developers normally set an easily maintainable location as the workspace. However, this practice causes the above problem when using an Emulator.

Another common practice is selecting a project and pressing Ctrl+1 to run the application in the Emulator. However, this requires the IDE to first synchronize the project before running the application, which causes delay and occasionally errors.

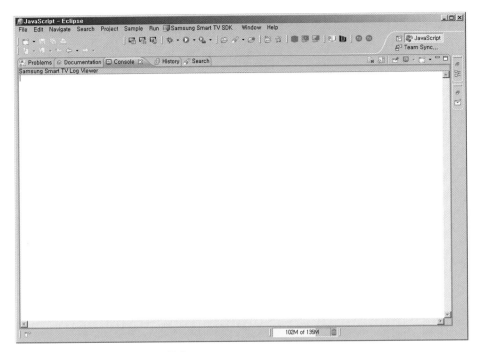

Figure 3-10. Application IDE - Eclipse

Configuring the Apache Folder

Apache web server's installation folder must be entered into the SDK to locally publish an application. Please skip the next step if this was done by default.

To configure the Apache folder, select "Samsung SmartTV SDK > Samsung SmartTV SDK Preference" in the order from the Eclipse's top menu bar. Then enter the Apache folder in the "Root Folder" option on the "Apache" tab.

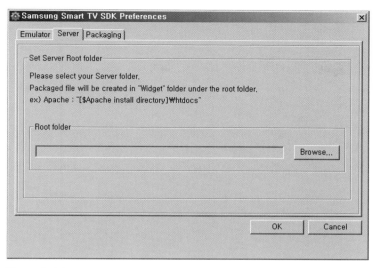

Figure 3-11. Configuring the Apache Folder in the SDK

Summary

The Samsung SmartTV SDK can be downloaded at the SDF. Although the Samsung SmartTV SDK supports multiple operating systems, it is recommended to use a Windows environment. The download includes the SDK IDE, an Emulator, and the Apache web server. There are a few additional configurations to set up, such as setting the Apache folder and the workspace, after installing the SDK.

04

Hello TV!

Before jumping into the Samsung SmartTV functions and APIs, let's make a simple "Hello TV!" application to briefly cover the whole application development process from creating a new project to publishing it.

Creating a New Project

Creating a New Project

The first step of developing a Samsung SmartTV application is creating a project. Necessary components can be created in the new project, and then necessary source code can be entered into the components. A project can be created in the included Eclipse IDE. See the following steps for the details.

Select the "Create Samsung SmartTV JavaScript App Project" submenu from the "Samsung SmartTV SDK" top menu of the Eclipse.

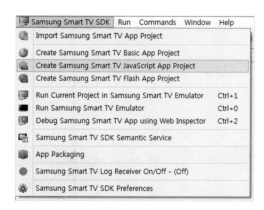

Figure 4-1. Selecting the JavaScript App Project

Select the menu to open the next window, where the project name, path, and application resolution can be entered.

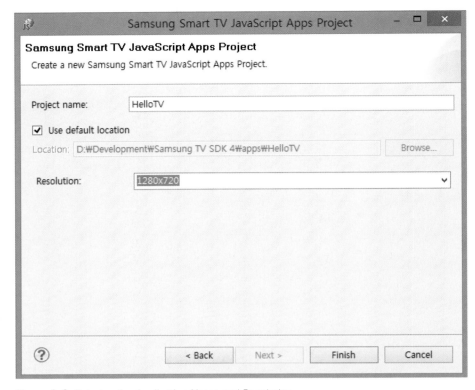

Figure 4-2. Entering the Application Name and Resolution

Click the "Finish" button to finish creating a new project step. The newly created project includes an "app" folder that contains a JavaScript file and a CSS file, "icon" folder that contains the application's icon, and an "images" folder to store image files used in the project. Index.html file, widget.info (holds resolution information) file, and config.xml (holds application's configuration information) files are stored in the root folder. The config.xml file will be discussed in depth later. See Figure 4-3 for an actual project structure.

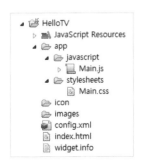

Figure 4-3. Structure of a Project

Runtime Configuration

Before testing to see if the first project will run, you need to set a path for an Emulator to run the application. Select the "Samsung SmartTV SDK Preferences" submenu from the "Samsung SmartTV SDK" top menu of the Eclipse.

Figure 4-4. Configuring the Emulator Path

Select the "Emulator" tab and configure the Emulator version for the Eclipse project. This function allows testing an application in various TV models. In addition, the "Emulator Font" option allows customizing display text font for the Emulator. Configure SDK's installation path at the "SDK Install Path" option. Normally, the correct path is already entered as the default, but manual configuration is necessary in some systems.

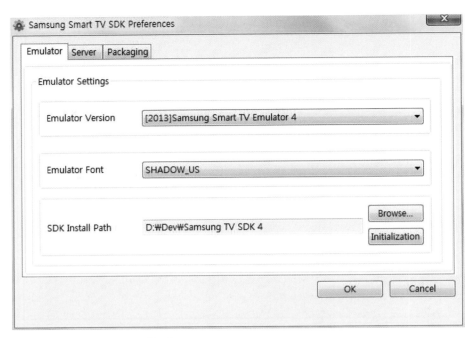

Figure 4-5. Configuring the Emulator

Next to the "Emulator" tab is the "Server" tab, which was explained in the previous chapter. This needs to be set up only once after installing the SDK, and it will not be covered in this chapter.

Executing the Project

An Emulator is needed to test a project. Select the project in the left pane's "Project Explorer," and click the "Run Current Project in Samsung SmartTV Emulator" submenu in the "Samsung SmartTV SDK" top menu of the Eclipse.

Figure 4-6. Executing a Project

The Emulator will then run the project. Note that there are two options, the "Run Current Project in Samsung SmartTV Emulator" and "Run Samsung SmartTV Emulator" submenus under the "Samsung SmartTV SDK" top menu. The first one runs the currently selected source code, and the latter opens up on its own. The latter option requires manual selection of a project to execute it.

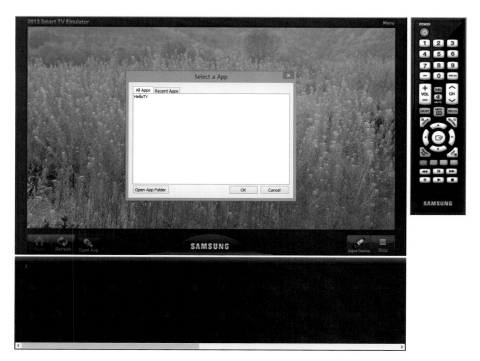

Figure 4-7. A Samsung SmartTV Emulator Window

config.xml

The config.xml file is automatically generated when a new project is created and holds the application's meta information, including environment, type, icon, and version. See below for its structure.

```xml
<?xml version="1.0" encoding="UTF-8"?>
<widget>
    <cpname itemtype="string"></cpname>
    <cplogo itemtype="string"></cplogo>
    <cpauthjs itemtype="string"></cpauthjs>
    <ThumbIcon itemtype="string">icon/sampleIcon_106_87.png</ThumbIcon>
    <BigThumbIcon itemtype="string">icon/sampleIcon_115_95.png</BigThumbIcon>
    <ListIcon itemtype="string">icon/sampleIcon_85_70.png</ListIcon>
    <BigListIcon itemtype="string">icon/sampleIcon_95_78.png</BigListIcon>
    <category itemtype="string"></category>
    <autoUpdate itemtype="boolean">n</autoUpdate>
    <ver itemtype="string">0.100</ver>
    <mgrver itemtype="string"></mgrver>
    <fullwidget itemtype="boolean">y</fullwidget>
    <type itemtype="string">user</type>
    <srcctl itemtype="boolean">y</srcctl>
    <ticker itemtype="boolean">n</ticker>
    <childlock itemtype="boolean">n</childlock>
    <videomute itemtype="boolean">n</videomute>
    <dcont itemtype="boolean">y</dcont>
    <widgetname itemtype="string">HelloTV</widgetname>
    <description itemtype="string">Description of application</description>
    <width itemtype="string">1280</width>
    <height itemtype="string">720</height>
    <author itemtype="group">
        <name itemtype="string">Handstudio Co., Ltd.</name>
        <email itemtype="string">tv@mhand.net</email>
        <link itemtype="string">http://handstudio.net</link>
        <organization itemtype="string">handstudio Co., Ltd.</organization>
    </author>
</widget>
```

It is not necessary to review every line of the preceding example code. But important items are described in the following table.

Component	Description	Value
<ThumbIcon> <BigThumbIcon> <ListIcon> <BigListIcon>	Application icon's path to be shown on a SmartTV. Pixel size for each option: ThumbIcon [106 x 87], BigThumbIcon [115 x 95], ListIcon [85 x 70], BigListIcon [95 x 78].	File Path
<category>	Application's Category VOD, sports, game, lifestyle, information, education	String
<autoUpdate>	Automatic Update when Connected to a Smart Hub	y | n
<ver>	Application Version. Server computer updates an application according to its version information.	x.xxx
<fullwidget>	Affects on Using Full-Screen and Audio Policy	y | n
<widgetname>	Application's Name	String
<description>	Application's Brief Description	String
<width><height>	Application's Width and Height	Number
<author>	Content Author's Contact Information - name: Name of the Author - email: E-mail Address of the Author - link: Website Address of the Author - organization: Organization Name of the Author	string

Table 4-1. Components of a config.xml File

The config.xml file defines an application's type. The previously mentioned application manager obtains an application version and execution information through this config.xml file. Note that an error in the config.xml file may cause the application to fail. Consult the SDF to obtain descriptions for items not described in the preceding table.

▶ Note: http://www.samsungdforum.com/Guide/art00011/index.html

Implementing the Hello TV! Program

Entire Source Code

Let's put the detailed API information aside and look at how an actual application is implemented. This simple "Hello TV!" project will be used to briefly explain how required HTML, JavaScript, and CSS files are implemented with the actual source code. The "Hello TV!" is an application that displays text information based on remote control directional keys input. The entire source code of the "Hello TV!" project is displayed below.

index.html

```html
<!DOCTYPE html>
<html>
    <head>
        <meta http-equiv="Content-Type" content="text/html; charset=utf-8">
        <title>HelloTV</title>

        <!-- TODO : Common API -->
        <script type="text/javascript" language="javascript" src="$MANAGER_
WIDGET/Common/API/Widget.js"></script>
        <script type="text/javascript" language="javascript" src="$MANAGER_
WIDGET/Common/API/TVKeyValue.js"></script>

        <!-- TODO : Javascript code -->
        <script language="javascript" type="text/javascript" src="app/
javascript/Main.js"></script>

        <!-- TODO : Style sheets code -->
        <link rel="stylesheet" href="app/stylesheets/Main.css" type="text/
css">
    </head>

    <body onload="Main.onLoad();" onunload="Main.onUnload();">
        <!-- Dummy anchor as focus for key events -->
        <a href="javascript:void(0);" id="anchor" onkeydown="Main.keyDown();"></
a>
```

```
        <!-- TODO: your code here -->
        <label id="hello">HelloTV</label>
    </body>
</html>
```

```
var widgetAPI = new Common.API.Widget(); // Create a Common Module API.
var tvKey = new Common.API.TVKeyValue(); // Initialize a tvKey object that
holds all remote control events.
var Main ={};

Main.onLoad = function(){
    this.enableKeys();
    widgetAPI.sendReadyEvent();
};

Main.onUnload = function(){
};

Main.enableKeys = function(){
    document.getElementById("anchor").focus(); // Give focus to an anchor.
};

Main.keyDown = function(){
    var keyCode = event.keyCode; // Receive the key value if a remote control
event is sensed.

    switch(keyCode){ // Declare an event to execute based on the received
remote control key value.
        case tvKey.KEY_RETURN:
            widgetAPI.sendReturnEvent(); // Send "return" message to the
application manager. The application is ended and control is returned to the
Smart Hub.

            break;
        case tvKey.KEY_LEFT:
```

```
            document.getElementById("hello").innerHTML = "LEFT"; // Set the
Element with id "hello" to "LEFT"
            break;
        case tvKey.KEY_RIGHT:
            document.getElementById("hello").innerHTML = "RIGHT"; // Set the
Element with id "hello" to "RIGHT"
            break;
        case tvKey.KEY_UP:
            break;
        case tvKey.KEY_DOWN:
            break;
        case tvKey.KEY_ENTER:
            break;
        default:
            alert("Unhandled key");
            break;
    }
};
```

Main.css

```
* {
    padding: 0;
    margin: 0;
    border: 0;
}

body {
    width: 1280px;
    height: 720px;
    background-color: #FFF;
}

#hello {
    font-size: 250px;
}
```

A SmartTV application's index.html file is loaded first by the App Engine, similar to when a website is loaded by a web browser. Therefore, a SmartTV application's index.html also needs to declare the necessary JavaScript and CSS files, as shown below.

index.html

```
<script language="javascript" type="text/javascript" src="app/javascript/Main.js"></script>
<link rel="stylesheet" href="app/stylesheets/Main.css" type="text/css">
```

Preparation to Run an Application

The sendReadyEvent() function is used to send a "ready" message from the Application Manager to run the application. This function also initializes necessary plug-ins and the Common Module API.

```
var widgetAPI = new Common.API.Widget(); // Create a Common Module API.
widgetAPI.sendReadyEvent(); // Send "ready" message to the Application Manager.
```

The Application Manager

The Application Manager provides the Common Module API that configures the application to the TV environment. This module includes functions that install, run, and delete a Samsung SmartTV application, as well as the SSO (Single Sign-On) application account information transferring module. It also senses and recognizes remote control events, and manages files created by the File API.

Loading the Initialization

After an application is started, an internal browser loads the index.html file. To call the sendReadEvent() function shown above, and load the actual application, a handler must be registered to call the function. The HTML onload handler is registered to the body tag for this purpose.

```
<body onload="Main.onLoad();">
```

Handling Remote Key Events

To handle remote control key events, load the TVKeyValue JavaScript library in the Common Module API, as shown below.

index.html

```
<script type="text/javascript" language="javascript" src="$MANAGER_WIDGET/
Common/API/TVKeyValue.js"></script>
```

The TVKeyValue library is loaded to call remote control event handling functions of the Common Module API. The API's Common.API.TVKeyValue object is used to initialize the tvKey object that includes all remote control event members, as shown below.

Main.js

```
// Create an Instance of Common Module API.
var tvKey = new Common.API.TVKeyValue()
```

Create an anchor element to handle a remote control event as shown next. This anchor includes the onKeyDown handler. Please see chapter 5, Focus, for detailed information how the element receives focus.

```
<a href="javascript:void(0);" id="anchor" onkeydown="Main.keyDown();"></a>
```

The next step will implement the Main.keyDown() function, which is registered as the onKeyDown handler for the above "anchor." "anchor" is a dummy anchor created to receive remote control key events while it has the focus. Main. keyDown receives the event.keyCode parameter and uses a switch statement to compare it with tvKey values and execute the proper reaction.

Main.js

```
// Called by onload handler of body element.
Main.onload = function(){
    Main.enableKeys();
};


// Focuses on anchor element with id "anchor"
Main.enableKeys = function() {
    document.getElementById("anchor").focus();
};


// Event handler for an anchor element.
Main.keyDown = function(){
    var keyCode = event.keyCode;

    switch(keyCode){
        case tvKey.KEY_RETURN:
            widgetAPI.sendReturnEvent();
            break;
        case tvKey.KEY_LEFT:
            document.getElementById("hello").innerHTML = "LEFT";
            break;
        case tvKey.KEY_RIGHT:
            document.getElementById("hello").innerHTML = "RIGHT";
            break;
        case tvKey.KEY_UP:
            break;
```

```
        case tvKey.KEY_DOWN:
            break;
        case tvKey.KEY_ENTER:
            break;
        default:
            alert("Unhandled key");
            break;
    }
};
```

When the application is executed, the Main.onload function is first called by the Main.onload handler. Then the Main.onload function gives focus to the anchor using the Main.enableKeys function.

Closing an Application

Follow these steps to close an application:

- Remote control back key or Exit key is pressed.

- The sendExitEvent function or sendReturnEvent function is called to send the event to the Application Manager, which transfers control back to the broadcasted program screen or the Smart Hub.

- The sendExitEvent and sendReturnEvent may be called by a Common Module API member object, Widget.

Running Hello TV!

See below for the "Hello TV!" application running on the Emulator.

Figure 4-8. Running the "Hello TV!" Application

Press the Left directional key on the virtual remote controller of the Emulator to see the text changing into "LEFT."

Figure 4-9. Left Directional Key of the Virtual Remote Controller Is Pressed

Now, press the Right directional key to see the text change again.

Figure 4-10. Right Directional Key of the Virtual Remote Controller Is Pressed

Installing Hello TV! on a TV

Now let's install the user-created application on a Samsung SmartTV to test and debug it in a real environment. The Emulator and an actual SmartTV environment have some differences in system environment and engine implementation. It is best to always test an application on a real TV before publishing it.

Application Packaging

Simple checking and testing of an application can be done on the Emulator without packaging. But an application needs to be packaged to be published or tested on a SmartTV. See the following steps on how the packaging is done.

01. Select the project to package on the Project Explorer.

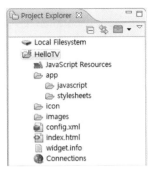

Figure 4-11. Selecting a Project to Package

02. Select the "App Packaging" submenu on the "Samsung SmartTV SDK" top menu of the Eclipse.

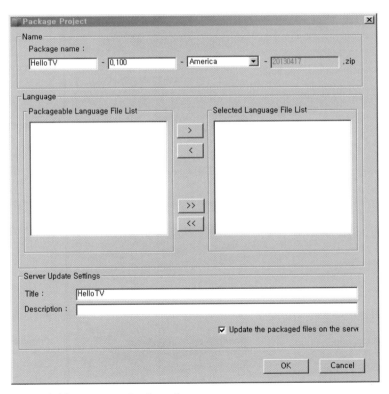

Figure 4-12. Packaging Configuration

03. Enter necessary information for the App Packaging.

The App Packaging window has the following options:

- Name: Enter the application name, version, and country where the application will be used. Enter the project name, then the <ver> tag value from the config.xml file will be entered as the default. This value is used for filenames of the package.
- Language: Used for an application that supports multiple languages.
- Server Update Settings: Check the "Update the packaged files on the server" box to upload the package to the server. Enter the title and description. These values will be shown when installing the application. The description can be skipped.

Figure 4-13. Pop-up Window that Shows Packaging Completion

04. Confirm the Packaging Completion pop-up message.

When the packaging is complete, a message with the installation file path will be shown. The packaging file is created in the <SDK Installation Path>\ Package folder, and the same file will be copied into the <Apache Installation Path>\Widget if the web server update box is checked. The information file for the copied package is saved in the <Apache Installation Path>\widgetlist. xml file.

Application Publishing Information

Once the application packaging is complete, it can be installed on a SmartTV using the IP address of the server. The SmartTV reads the widgetlist.xml from the Apache web server and obtains application package file location and other meta information.

widgetlist.xml

```xml
<?xml version="1.0" encoding="UTF-8" standalone="no"?>
<rsp stat="ok">
    <list>
        <widget id="HelloTV">
            <title>HelloTV</title>
            <compression size="2711" type="zip" />
            <description />
            <download>http://192.168.0.6/Widget/HelloTV_0.100_
America_20130211.zip</download>
        </widget>
    </list>
</rsp>
```

The widgetlist.xml has an application title and description entered by the user during the packaging process, as well as package file size and path. Users can package and upload multiple applications to a SmartTV at the same time. The completed packaging information on the widgetlist.xml is not deleted and only updated during repackaging. Therefore, unused application information needs to be manually deleted from the widgetlist.xml file, unfortunately, using a text editor.

Summary

Before discussing the Samsung SmartTV functions and APIs, a simple project was demonstrated to show an entire application development cycle, including project creation, implementation, execution, and publication. Note that not-yet-covered scene and focus were used. But do not worry about them. Instead, try to understand the rough development cycle. Scene and focus will be discussed in detail in later chapters.

05

Focus

Anchor and Focus

Anchor elements are often used to navigate between HTML pages in a web service. However, it is used for a somewhat different purpose in a general SmartTV application. An anchor is capable of focusing an element in addition to navigating among pages using the href property. This property is often used in SmartTV applications to control scenes.

In a SmartTV application, HTML/JavaScript focus is used to select and mark one of several items simultaneously displayed on the screen. Try to re-call using remote control directional keys (up/down/left/right) to focus different items on a SmartTV or a set-top box type IPTV service, in which the OK key activates the focused content.

Anchors and focuses are the fundamental tools of controlling a Samsung SmartTV application using a remote controller. Gesture Recognition has been added recently to allow more freedom in moving focus and selecting content with hand movement.

Registering/Unregistering a Remote Control Key

Registering a remote control key means that the application will have its own functions to handle the key input. Unregistering a key means using a SmartTV's default OSD (On Screen Display) functions to handle it. When an application is executed, basic remote control keys (directional keys and the OK key) are automatically registered for the application to use. To return control of a registered key to the basic OSD, the key can be unregistered. See the following remote control volume key example to help understand this concept.

If an application is a FullWidget app, volume keys are automatically registered when the application is executed. To allow users to use volume keys' original TV OSD function of controlling volume, those keys need to be unregistered by the application. To use the volume up key for another function (such as controlling an application's internal gage), the KEY_VOL_UP key event needs to be registered in the application and controlled by a custom event handling for the KEY_VOL_UP event.

Commonly used keys are automatically registered when an app is executed to relieve developers. Just remember to unregister a key event if you want to return control of the key to the original OSD functions of a TV.

The SDF provides various APIs for registering and unregistering the keys.

Here is a sample source code that registers the KEY_TOOLS key.

```
// Create a plug-in instance of the Common Module API.
var pluginAPI = new Common.API.Plugin();


Main.onLoad = function() {
    window.onShow = onShowEvent;
    widgetAPI.sendReadyEvent();
};


onShowEvent = function() {

    // Register TOOLS key.
    pluginAPI.registKey(tvKey.KEY_TOOLS);
};
```

The SDF also provides an API that registers multiple keys simultaneously. See the following example that registers multiple keys that are used by a FullWidget type application.

```
// Create a plug-in instance of the Common Module API.
var pluginAPI = new Common.API.Plugin();


Main.onLoad = function() {
```

```
    window.onShow = onShowEvent;
    widgetAPI.sendReadyEvent();
};


onShowEvent = function() {

    // Register all keys that are used by a FullWidget type application.
    pluginAPI.registFullWidgetKey();
};
```

Now let's see how unregistering is implemented. The next example unregisters volume up/down keys and mute keys so that the original TV OSD function can be used.

```
// Create a plug-in instance of the Common Module API.
var pluginAPI = new Common.API.Plugin();

Main.onLoad = function() {
    window.onShow = onShowEvent;
    widgetAPI.sendReadyEvent();
};


onShowEvent = function() {
    var nnaviPlugin = document.getElementById('pluginObjectNNavi');
    naviPlugin.SetBannerState(1);

    // Unregister keys for volume OSD.
    pluginAPI.unregistKey(tvKey.KEY_VOL_UP);
    pluginAPI.unregistKey(tvKey.KEY_VOL_DOWN);
    pluginAPI.unregistKey(tvKey.KEY_MUTE);
};
```

It is more logical to register and unregister remote control keys during application initialization by placing them within the body.onload function. But the example source code shows that they are placed within the window.onShow function that is called after the body.onload function. This is to avoid any conflict that may occur when key registering and unregistering for the Smart Hub and for the application execution. Using the window.onShow function guarantees that the Smart Hub's processes are already completed.

Note that only a few keys are automatically registered except on a full-screen application. All the necessary keys need to be manually registered.

Handling Remote Control Events

Remote control key codes are mapped into JavaScript codes that switch focus between elements, by assigning an appropriate process to each of the registered key events. See the following table for a list of registered key values, for both a full-screen application and a single-wide application (ticker).

Full-Screen Application		Single-Wide Application (Ticker)
KEY_VOL_UP	KEY_1	KEY_WHEELDOWN
KEY_VOL_DOWN	KEY_2	KEY_WHEELUP
KEY_MUTE	KEY_3	KEY_RED
KEY_TOOLS	KEY_4	KEY_GREEN
KEY_INFO	KEY_5	KEY_YELLOW
KEY_EMODE	KEY_6	KEY_BLUE
KEY_DMA	KEY_7	KEY_RW
KEY_MENU	KEY_8	KEY_PAUSE
KEY_SOURCE	KEY_9	KEY_FF
KEY_PRECH	KEY_0	KEY_PLAY
KEY_FAVCH	KEY_WHEELDOWN	KEY_STOP
KEY_CHLIST	KEY_WHEELUP	KEY_ENTER

Full-Screen Application		Single-Wide Application (Ticker)
KEY_DMA	KEY_RED	KEY_RETURN
KEY_TTX_MIX	KEY_GREEN	KEY_EXIT
KEY_GUIDE	KEY_YELLOW	
KEY_SUBTITLE	KEY_BLUE	
KEY_ASPECT	KEY_RW	
KEY_DOLBY_SRR	KEY_PAUSE	
KEY_MTS	KEY_FF	
KEY_PANEL_CH_UP	KEY_PLAY	
KEY_PANEL_CH_DOWN	KEY_STOP	
KEY_PANEL_VOL_UP	KEY_ENTER	
KEY_PANEL_VOL_DOWN	KEY_RETURN	
KEY_PANEL_ENTER	KEY_EXIT	
KEY_PANEL_SOURCE		
KEY_PANEL_MENU		

Table 5-1. Key Event List for Different Application Types

If an application has a handler and an assigned function for a KEY_UP event, it will process efficiently when a user presses the Up key of the remote controller. But nothing will happen if the application is not programmed to handle the KEY_UP event.

Let's see an example source code for the preceding case. The following example will handle the most commonly used four directional keys, back key, and OK key events. First, add an anchor element to handle the key events.

```
<!—Anchor element to handle four directional keys, back key, and ok key. -->
<a href="javascript:void(0);" id="anchor" onkeydown="Main.keyDown();"></a>
```

The anchor element must have an href property, but any value assigned for this property will cause the browser to open a new page with the value as its address. That is an unnecessary function for the scene-based development method of this book, and can be blocked by calling the void(0) function that always returns null value.

The currently focused anchor will use the onkeydown handler to process the event generated when a SmartTV user presses a remote control key. The handler calls the function if there is a registered function for the event.

The following example uses an event-handling function to process the four directional keys, the Back key, and the OK key, which are received by the previously defined anchor.

```
// Create a TVKeyValue instance of the Common Module API.
var tvKey = new Common.API.TVKeyValue();

// Event handling function registered on the anchor's handler.
Main.keyDown = function () {
    var keyCode = event.keyCode;

    switch (keyCode) {
        case tvKey.KEY_LEFT:
            break;
        case tvKey.KEY_RIGHT:
            break;
        case tvKey.KEY_UP:
            break;
        case tvKey.KEY_DOWN:
            break;
        case tvKey.KEY_ENTER:
            break;
        case tvKey.KEY_RETURN:
            break;
    }
};
```

See the variable tvKey on the source code. This is an instance of the Common Module API library TVKeyValue.js. All remote control key code values are saved in this object as member properties.

Also, note the object type global variable event.keyCode, which stores the last pressed remote control key value. This value is passed to the local variable keyCode, then is used by a switch statement to process four directional keys, ok key, and return key inputs. The switch statement ignores any other keys.

While there are many key codes, memorizing them is not necessary because only a few common keys will be used by most applications. Visit the SDF for detailed information about the remote control events.

▶ Note: http://samsungdforum.com/Guide/art00046/index.html

Moving the Focus

As shown, placing the browser focus on an anchor element, to handle remote control key events and navigate between scenes, is the fundamental design concept of this book. The example uses only one anchor element for an easier demonstration. But commercial applications use many interacting anchor elements that pass the focus back and forth. Understanding this concept is essential for a SmartTV application developer.

Before covering the focus moving in detail, let's clearly define a UI component and an anchor element. A UI component is commonly shown on the screen as a menu button or a content image thumbnail, and is a displayed element. An anchor element is an HTML <a> tag that handles remote-control events and actually receives focus. To implement a natural focus system with distinct styles, these anchor elements and UI components must be defined.

See the next example that shows focus movement between two elements, "left" and "right."

```
<!--Left element -- >
<div id="left">
    <a href="javascript:void(0);" id="left_anchor" onkeydown="left.
keyDown();">left</a>
</div>

<!--Right element -- >
<div id="right">
    <a href="javascript:void(0);" id="right_anchor" onkeydown="right.
keyDown();">right</a>
</div>
```

```
var tvKey = new Common.API.TVKeyValue();

var left = {};
var right = {};

// Left anchor event handling function
left.keyDown = function()
{
    var keyCode = event.keyCode;

    switch(keyCode)
    {
        case tvKey.KEY_RIGHT:
            jQuery('#right_anchor').focus();     // Right anchor focus
            jQuery('#right').addClass('focus');
            jQuery('#left').removeClass('focus');
            break;
        default:
            break;
    }
};
```

```javascript
// Right anchor event handling function
right.keyDown = function()
{
    var keyCode = event.keyCode;

    switch(keyCode)
    {
        case tvKey.KEY_LEFT:
            jQuery('#left_anchor').focus();    // Left anchor focus
            jQuery('#left').addClass('focus');
            jQuery('#right').removeClass('focus');
            break;
        default:
            break;
    }
};
```

```css
#left{
    display:inline-block;
    float: left;
    width: 200px;
    height: 200px;
}

#left.focus{
    background-color: blue;
}

#right{
    display:inline-block;
    float: right;
    width: 200px;
    height: 200px;
}
```

```
#right.focus{
    background-color: blue;
}
```

Styles need to be modified to visually indicate which element is currently focused. See the above Main.css source code that has added a ".focus" class that was used to modify the background style. Note that each element's class is controlled by the jQuery. The source code does not specify the initial focus. But if the left anchor is focused, the remote controller's right directional key event will move the focus to the right anchor. With the focus movement, the UI component paired with the newly focused anchor will be modified by adding the .focus class using the jQuery's addClass function. The previous anchor's UI component will also be modified by removing the .focus class. This practice visually indicates the focus movement with the style element.

Handling a Mouse Event

Let's briefly review the new mouse event supported since Samsung SmartTV 2012 models. An application can be configured to support mouse input using a mouse element in the config.xml file, as shown below.

```
<mouse itemtype="string">y</mouse>
```

The Smart Interaction's gesture recognition feature works like the mouse event. Details will be covered in chapter 13, Advanced Features – SI Gesture Recognition.

When both a Remote Controller and a Mouse are used together

This book focuses on event handling with remote controller-based anchors, and mouse events are used together only in special cases. This is to avoid a browser's basic tendency of moving the focus to a mouse-clicked element that causes unintentionally losing anchor focus for a random mouse click. When a mouse clicks an element that either does not need to or should not have the focus, the focus is unintentionally moved to the element, which causes the remote controller to lose navigation capability.

To solve the problem, the anchor-based event-handling method needs to be modified. One way would be processing the onkeydown handler in the <body> tag instead of in an anchor.

```
<body onload="Main.onLoad();" onunload="Main.onUnload();" onkeydown="Main.
keyDown();">
```

This allows the top-most body element to handle the events and solves the focus-losing problem. Many different solutions are suitable for different situations.

Summary

A SmartTV application uses the focus feature as its primary navigation tool. This is implemented using anchors. Using the focus on an anchor allows an application to process remote-control key events. Also, a focused anchor's UI component needs to have a distinct UI style. Be careful not to mishandle the focus and create bad user interface. No amount of useful content will compensate for it.

06

Scenes-Based Display Design

A Samsung SmartTV application runs on a browser environment that is similar to PC-based web browsers, and can use most of the standard web development techniques. Chapter 6 will introduce and carefully review a scenes-based programming method that uses different scenes to efficiently handle key events. This method accommodates characteristics of a TV application that uses remote controller-generated KeyDown events.

The Samsung SmartTV SDK provides the Scene Manager to quickly and easily develop an application screen. However, in this chapter, we will not use the Scene Manager; instead, we will manually implement a simple TV app screen. This will help us to understand how a SmartTV application handles possible exceptions.

This chapter's scene creation / switch method is not the ultimate right answer. Different situations require different solutions. Please consider the next method as a tutorial that will help you understand the structure of a Samsung SmartTV application.

Scenes-Based Design

As explained earlier, a Samsung SmartTV application consists of HTML, CSS, and JavaScript files, as does a web application. Therefore, we can use styles and HTML elements, as is commonly done in web development.

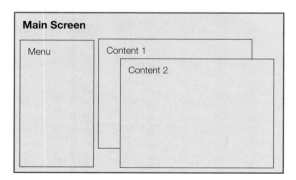

Figure 6-1. Scenes Structure

While a website treats each HTML page as a unit display, a Samsung SmartTV application treats each div element as a unit scene. Therefore, a TV application screen often has multi-layered scenes.

index.html

```
<!-- scene 1 element -->
<div id="scene1" class="scene">
    <!-- scene 1 anchor>
    <a href="javascript:void(0);" class="handler" onkeydown=" Scene1.
keyDown();"></a>
</div>
```

The div element with ID "scene1" is one of the display layers used below. Note that "scene1" has an anchor. This anchor is focused when "scene1" is activated. A focused anchor is triggered by remote control key events. Although different anchor-focus techniques are available, assigning a unique anchor for each scene is always a good practice. It becomes increasingly harder to control an entire application with just one anchor as the application structure becomes more complex with complicated focus-key events. Please review chapter 5, Focus, for further explanation of anchor and focus.

Unlike a web application in a browsing environment on a PC, a Samsung SmartTV application uses the remote control as its main user interface. See the Remote Control Key Guide to learn how remote control key events are defined. Samsung SmartTV's navigation policy (Key Guide) can be found on the SDF and is also explained in chapter 5.

Main.css

```
body {
    margin: 0;
    padding: 0;
}

/* Define common styles for all scenes */
div.scene {
```

```css
    position: absolute;
    top: 0;
    left: 0;
    width: 100%;
    height: 100%;
    /* all scenes are hidden until focused */
    display: none;
}


/* define individual styles for each scene */
#scene1{

  ...

}
```

The CSS file defines both common and individual scene styles. It also defines the navigation icon styles for remote control keys, which are used by scenarios of all scenes.

scene.js

```javascript
// instance of necessary elements by scene 1
var Scene1 =
{
    elem: null,
    handler: null
};


// initialize necessary elements and anchor by scene 1
Scene1.init = function ()
{
    this.elem = jQuery('#scene1');
    this.handler = this.elem.find('a');

    Scene1.init = function(){};
};


Scene1.show = function ()
{
```

```
        this.elem.show();
};

Scene1.hide = function ()
{
    this.elem.hide();
};

Scene1.focus = function ()
{
    this.handler.focus();
};

Scene1.load = function ()
{
    this.init();
};

Scene1.unload = function ()
{
    this.hide();
};
```

The scene.js needs to define functions to be used by each scene's scenario. The example code uses the most basic functions, including load, focus, show, and unload. The next functions can be used to focus on scene 1.

```
Scene1.load();
Scene1.show();
Scene1.focus();
```

First, use the load function to activate scene 1.

```
Scene1.load = function ()
{
    alert('Scene1 load');
```

```
        this.init();
    };
```

The Scene1.load function calls the Scene1.init function to initialize necessary elements. When it is complete, call the Scene.show function to display the scene.

```
Scene1.show = function ()
{
    alert('Scene1 show');
    this.elem.show();
};
```

The above code will display scene 1. The Scene1.show function was intentionally separated from the load function so that it could be independently used to switch between scenes. Like the show function, the focus function is also better when used independently. Note that the show function is called before the focus function. Scene1.elem has "none" as its display value before the this.show function is called. Because Scene1.handler is its subelement, the Scene1.focus function called before the show function is unable to keep the focus for scene 1.

```
Scene1.unload = function ()
{
    this.hide();
};
```

The Scene1.unload function is called to deactivate scene 1 and go back to the higher level scene or activate another subscene. While the Scene1.unload only calls Scene1.hide in turn, additional work may be necessary in addition to hiding it, depending on scene 1's scenario. Also, there can be different unload events for activating another subscene and going back to the higher level scene.

Switching Between Scenes

When the index.html file is loaded into the SmartTV's internal browser, the first scene will be displayed on the TV screen according to the application scenario. The activated scene will dominate the focus. If a user moves the focus and selects another scene, then the application activates the new scene and deactivates the previous scene. The activated scene is displayed and the deactivated scene is hidden. Many other methods can be used to switch scenes on a SmartTV, such as using dynamic layers or pop-up style sublayers. Be careful not to open too many unnecessary scenes; conserve limited physical memory capacity of a TV.

When a scene is switched, the focus also must be moved. Be careful not to lose the focus by switching to no existing scene, or to a scene of which its parent element is hidden.

The next example shows switching between the GalleryScene and its sublayer, SurveyScene.

gallery.js

```
GalleryScene.load = function()
{
    // GalleryScene
};


GalleryScene.keyDown = function()
{
    var keyCode = event.keyCode;
    switch(keyCode)
    {
        // Activate SurveyScene
        case tvKey.KEY_ENTER:
            SurveyScene.load();
            SurveyScene.show();
            SurveyScene.focus();
            break;
    }
};
```

Pressing the OK key while the GalleryScene is activated will activate the SurveyScene. Then the SurveyScene will be displayed on the SmartTV screen and the SurveyScene's member anchor will be focused.

survey.js

```
SurveyScene.load = function()
{
};


SurveyScene.keyDown = function()
{
    var keyCode = event.keyCode;
    switch(keyCode)
    {
        case tvKey.KEY_RETURN:
            widgetAPI.blockNavigation();  // Prevent application closing

            GalleryScene.load();
            GalleryScene.show();
            GalleryScene.focus();

            SurveyScene.unload();
            break;
    }
};
```

However, loading the upper level GalleryScene, as shown above, to return to the GalleryScene is not a good practice. The GalleryScene was only covered by the lower level SurveyScene. Simply transfer the focus back to the GalleryScene. Also, if the SurveyScene is shared by scenes other than the GalleryScene, directly controlling its upper-level scene may complicate the event handling. Then, how can the above code be improved?

Data Transfer Between Scenes

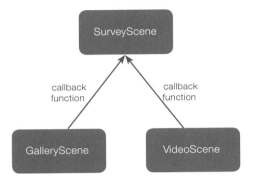

Figure 6-2. Data Transfer Between Scenes

The callback function can be used to easily share data and focus-related information while switching scenes.

```
GalleryScene.keyDown = function()
{
    var keyCode = event.keyCode;
    switch(keyCode)
    {
        case tvKey.KEY_ENTER:
            SurveryScene.load({
                onUnload : function(){
                    GalleryScene.focus();
                }
            });
              SurveyScene.show();
              SurveyScene.focus();
            break;
    }
};
SurveyScene.load = function(callback) {
    this.callback = jQuery.extend({}, {
        onUnload: function() {}
    }, callback);
};
```

```
SurveyScene.unload = function() {
    this.callback.onUnload();
};
```

In the above example, the SurveyScene is loaded with a callback function. It can then use the onUnload call function to return the focus to its upper-level GalleryScene. This practice is one of the safe handling methods in moving the focus: a TV application's vital function is that its exceptions must be properly handled.

The previous examples demonstrate simple scene switching and data transfer between scenes. Many different switching techniques are used in a production app, and there can be many exceptions to handle while transferring data. Making an independent object to manage shared functions and data among different scenes is another technique for efficient event management.

Summary

A Samsung SmartTV application can effectively use multi-layered scenes within an HTML page. There are other methods, such as using dynamic layers or fixed HTML pages, but a SmartTV's limited memory resources must be considered as well. Make sure that the target scene's parent element is visible while moving the focus. It is easier to have an independent module to manage different scenes in a complex application with difficult scene navigation and data transfer.

07

AV Player

The core purpose of a TV is to consume video content. The Samsung SmartTV supports both broadcasting programs and VOD content to be played in an application using its AVPlayer application library. This chapter will explain major APIs of the AV Player, and show how event functions are declared and called to control the player.

Initializing the AVPlayer Library

VOD-type applications are gaining popularity because they can maximize large screen features of the common SmartTV. The Samsung SmartTV supports two different approaches to play VOD content. The first method is using a standard web HTML tag, and the second method is using the AVPlayer included in the Samsung SmartTV Web Device API. See below for an example of playing contents with the HTML tag method.

```
<object src="http://www.w3schools.com/tags/movie.mp4" type="video/mp4"></object>
<video src="http://www.w3schools.com/tags/movie.mp4" type="video/mp4"></video>
<audio src="http://www.w3schools.com/tags/audio.mp3" type="audio/mp3"></audio>
```

While it is easy to implement the HTML tag approach, it has a drawback of severely limited player control other than the basic attributes supported by the HTML. Mainly, it cannot take advantage of using the focus policy to control player functions, or using callback functions to receive player events.

The following Web Device API's AV Player offers customized player control. This approach provides multiple playback methods and detailed contents controlling, by sending instructions to and receiving event messages from the AVPlayer library. See the next section for the initialization and the AVPlayer library, as well as the usage of the content-controlling functions and events.

Initializing the API

The following library needs to be declared before using the player API.

```
<script type="text/javascript" language="javascript" src="$MANAGER_WIDGET/
Common/webapi/1.0/webapis.js"></script>
```

The AV Player is part of the Web Device API that was declared above. This is much simpler than the previous player plug-in method, which required declaring the Plugin API and an object to hold the module.

Next, initialize the AV Player as, shown below.

```
var playerInstance = webapis.avplay;
playerInstance.getAVPlay(onAVPlayObtained, onGetAVPlayError);
```

The playerInstance object is used only to reference the AVPlayer library instance and call getAVPlay(). Then getAVPlayer() calls the onAVPlayerObtained() callback function, which loads the actual AVPlayer module. Another callback function, onGetAVPlayerError(), was also supplied for error handling.

```
var Main = {};

// Callback function to initialize the AVPlayer module
function onAVPlayObtained (avplay){
    Main.AVPlayer = avplay;
    Main.AVPlayer.init();
}

// Callback function for error handling while initializing the AVPlayer
module
function onGetAVPlayError(){
    alert('######onGetAVPlayError: ' + error.message);
}
```

The preceding code demonstrates an implementation of the callback functions to supply getAVPlay() as parameters. Note that the actual module loader, onAVPlayer(), receives the AVPlayer instance as its parameter. This instance is then bound to a local variable so that it can be accessed by all scenes (screen layers). Finally, init() is called to finalize the player initialization process.

Play, Pause, Stop, and Skip

The AVPlayer instance supports many API functions and basic player control events (play, pause, stop, skip) to control the player.

Type	Function	Description
Play	open(String url, AVPlayOption)	Initialize the player with a URL to load new content from
	play()	Play the loaded content
Control	pause()	Ppause the player
	resume()	Resume the player
	stop()	Stop the player
	jumpBackward(Number sec)	Jump backward for the parameter seconds and play
	jumpForward(Number sec)	Jump forward for the parameter seconds and play
Setup	setDisplayArea(Number x, Number y, Number width, Number height)	Set the player area starting from the (x, y) position to the parameter width and height
Information	duration	Display total content length
	videoWidth	Display current screen width of the player
	videoHeight	Display current screen height of the player

Table 7-1. Main Functions of the Player API

The preceding table only covers the most basic player controller APIs. See the following SDF link for the complete list of APIs.

▶ Note: http://www.samsungdforum.com/Guide/ref00008/avplay/dtv_avplay_module.html

Play

To play saved content, the player needs a path for the content. While the player can use both local and network media, streaming URL for network stored media is recommended. Absolute file path is required to play a locally stored media file. See the next example.

```
var playerInstance = deviceapis.avplay;
playerInstance.getAVPlay(onAVPlayObtained,onGetAVPlayError);

function onAVPlayObtained(avplay){
    Main.AVPlayer = avplay;
    Main.AVPlayer.init();
}

function onGetAVPlayError(){
    alert('######onGetAVPlayError: ' + error.message);
}

// load a media file
Main.AVPlayer.open("http://www.w3schools.com/tags/movie.mp4");

// play the content
Main.AVPlayer.play();
```

Once the AV Player is successfully initialized, use open() to set the URL for the playable content, then use play() to play the content.

The Samsung SmartTV supports the following media formats.

Type		Format	2012		2013	
			TV/AV	SDK 3.0	TV/AV	SDK 4.0
VOD	Streaming	HTTP	Supported	Supported	Supported	Supported
		HTTPS	Supported	Supported	Supported	Supported
		MMS	Supported	Supported	Supported	Supported
		RTP/RTSP	Supported	Supported	Supported	Supported
	Adaptive Streaming	Mpeg-Dash (xml metadata)	Supported OIPF Rel2 / MPEG2 TSonly / AES-128	Supported	Supported OIPF Rel2 / MPEG2 TSonly / AES-128	Supported
		HLS (m3u8 metadata)	Supported - v3	Supported - v3	Supported - v3	Supported - v3
		HLS audio	Supports High-Definition Audio with TS File Extension Only	Supports High-Definition Audio with TS File Extension Only	Supports High-Definition Audio with TS File Extension Only	Supports High-Definition Audio with TS File Extension Only

Table 7-2. Playable Media Formats on the Samsung SmartTV

The Samsung SmartTV also supports adaptive streaming technology that reduces buffering by automatically adopting to a client network environment with variable quality playbacks.

Player Pause and Stop

In addition to the play event, the pause and stop events are the most basic player control events. If a user presses the remote control stop or pause key, the player needs to correctly handle the user input. See the example for using stop() to stop a playback. The AVPlayer instance is already initialized.

```
// stop playback
Main.AVPlayer.stop();
```

The stop() function also needs to be called after completion of a playback. The AV Player provides onStreamCompleted() to handle the playback completion event.

The onStreamCompleted() function is included in the AVPlayerCallback API. See the SDF link for details.

▶ Note: http://www.samsungdforum.com/Guide/ref00008/avplay/dtv_avplay_avplaycallback.html

The pause() function works the same way.

```
// pause playback
Main.AVPlayer.pause();
```

The paused player needs to be resumed.

```
// resume paused playback
Main.AVPlayer.resume();
```

The preceding event functions can be called within the user key event handling code to create a working player with play, stop, and pause capabilities.

Skip

The AV Player supports skipping backward or forward in set seconds. It can be used to move playing content forward or backward for a specified amount of time. These functions are commonly bound to remote control ◄◄ and ►► buttons as their event-handling functions.

```
// jump 5 seconds backward from the current position
Main.AVPlayer.jumpBackward(5);

// jump 5 seconds forward from the current position
Main.AVPlayer.jumpForward(5);
```

Handling Remote Control Key Events

The next example demonstrates how an AVPlayer instance handles user remote control key events.

```
var Main = {};

function AVPlayerRun(){

    var playerInstance = deviceapis.avplay;
    playerInstance.getAVPlay(onAVPlayObtained, onGetAVPlayError);

    // initialize the AV Player using avplay instance
    function onAVPlayObtained(avplay){
        Main.AVPlayer = avplay;
        Main.AVPlayer.init();
    }

    function onGetAVPlayError(){
        alert('######onGetAVPlayError: ' + error.message);
    }

    // load and play a content file
    Main.AVPlayer.open("http://www.w3schools.com/tags/movie.mp4");
    Main.AVPlayer.play();
```

```
        jQuery("anchor_player").focus();
}



Main.player.keyDown = function()
{
    var keyCode = event.keyCode;
    switch(keyCode)
    {
        case tvKey.KEY_RETURN:
            Player.stop();
            Main.content.anchor.focus();
            break;
        case tvKey.KEY_PLAY:
            // resume the player
            Main.AVPlayer.resume();
            break;
        case tvKey.KEY_STOP:
            // stop the player
            Main.AVPlayer.stop();
            break;
        case tvKey.KEY_PAUSE:
            // pause the player
            Main.AVPlayer.pause();
            break;
        case tvKey.KEY_RW:
            // jump 5 seconds backward from the current position
            Main.AVPlayer.jumpBackward(5);
            break;
        case tvKey.KEY_FF:
            // jump 5 seconds forward from the current position
            Main.AVPlayer.jumpForward(5);
            break;
        default:
            break;
    }
};
```

AVPlayerRun() initializes the player and plays the content. Then it sets focus on the player anchor, so that remote control user inputs can be handled while playing. Note that the anchor's handler, Main.player.keyDown(), is calling an appropriate AVPlayer event function for each input key.

The SDF also supports many callback functions to handle specific player status, notably AVPlayCallback() that was mentioned with the player stop function, and BufferingCallback() and SubtitleDataCallback().

> ► Note: http://www.samsungdforum.com/Guide/ref00008/avplay/dtv_avplay_
> module.html

Utilizing the callback functions enables specialized interface, such as player-specific subtitles and the timeline.

Summary

The AVPlayer library function can be used to program powerful media player capability into an application. However, the current Samsung SmartTV can run only one instance of the AV Player, and network environment and TV capability may cause slow player loading time. Also, make sure that the intended content is compatible with the currently supported media formats, since the Samsung SmartTV has limited media format support.

08

Hands Frame Application 1 – Basic Version

Chapter 8 demonstrates implementing a simple browsing-type application, "Hands Frame," and reviews its functions. While the application has a basic design, it covers critical SmartTV application functions such as scene, focus, and player. Hands Frame is a gallery application that can browse various VOD content introducing Handstudio, the author organization of this book.

Briefly, the Hands Frame application has the following structure: The top header displays the company slogan and logo, the left side has a list of categories, and the right pane displays the currently focused category. All these are implemented on one main layer. There are more sublayers, such as company information that will be shown when the remote control Information key is pressed.

For creating and configuring a new project, refer to chapter 4, Hello TV! This chapter does not discuss that topic.

See the next figure for two screen shots of the Hands Frame application.

Figure 8-1. Hands Frame > Information Scene

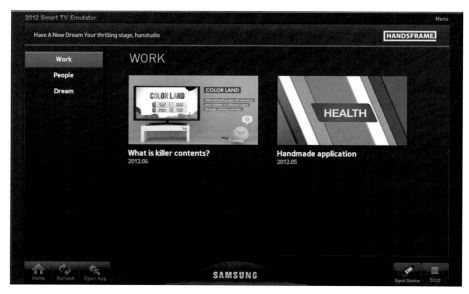

Figure 8-2. Hands Frame > Main > Work

Main Scene

Most of the functions of the Hands Frame application, including event handling, run on the main scene. The main scene consists of the left category menu pane, and the right contents pane.

Note that all HTML codes are in the index.html file, JavaScript codes are in the Main.js file, and styles are in the Main.css file.

First, declare a div element for the main scene in the index.html.

```
<div id="scene_main"></div>
```

Header

The header displays static information, including Handstudio's slogan and the application title. The header is not an independent scene and can be simply declared within the main scene.

```
<div id="scene_main">
    <div id="header"></div>
</div>
```

The header also does not need its own styles, since it is just an image file.

Category List

A common website uses a top- or left-menu navigation system that is activated by mouse click events to display appropriate content. A TV application uses the same UX, except that the menu focus replaces the mouse clicks. The Hands Frame uses the category list for its navigation menu.

As shown below, add the category element following the header element, in the index.html file.

```
<div id="scene_main" >
    <div id="header"></div>
    <div id="category">
        <ul>
            <li class="work">Work</li>
            <li class="people">People</li>
            <li class="dream">Dream</li>
        </ul>
    </div>
</div>

<a href="javascript:void(0);" id="anchor_category" onkeydown="Main.category.
keyDown();"></a>
```

The category element is an HTML <div> layer with a <ul> list. The list has three options, each with its own ID and class. Then an anchor for the category element is defined to handle focus and remote control key events.

Next, the following CSS defines styles of the category element.

```css
#category ul{
    list-style: none;
}

#category ul li{
    width: 235px;
    height: 50px;
    color: #fff;
    font-size:20px;
    line-height: 50px;
    text-align: center;
}

#category.focus ul li.focus{
    color: #fff;
    background: URL("../../images/btn_menu.png") top;
}

#category.focus ul li.selected{
    color: #c62ad3;
    background: URL("../../images/btn_menu.png") bottom;
}
```

Note that #category.focus ul li.focus was designed to have a distinguished style when it is focused. Note that .focus was declared twice. The first style was to distinguish the whole category menu scene from unfocused other scenes (header and contents), while the second style was to distinguish a selected menu item from the rest, within the category menu.

The category element is frequently used in the code. It is a good practice to assign an object member property of the Main variable, since the category scene is part of the main scene, to easily reference it.

```
var Main = {
    category : {
        elem : jQuery('#category'),
        li     : jQuery('#category').find('ul > li'),
        anchor : jQuery('#anchor_category'),
    }
};
```

In addition to the category element, an anchor element needs to be created to receive the focus for the category. Common elements are declared as member objects of Main for easier tracking.

The next event function handles key inputs while the category anchor is focused.

```
Main.category.keyDown = function()
{
    var keyCode = event.keyCode;

    switch(keyCode)
    {
        case tvKey.KEY_RETURN:
            widgetAPI.sendReturnEvent();
            break;
        case tvKey.KEY_RIGHT:
            break;
        case tvKey.KEY_UP:
            break;
        case tvKey.KEY_DOWN:
            break;
        case tvKey.KEY_INFO :
            break;
        default:
            alert("Unhandled key");
            break;
```

```
    }
};
```

If a remote key event is generated while the declared category anchor (id = "anchor_category") is focused, the onkeydown handler calls Main.category. keyDown().

Main.category.keyDown() obtains the remote key code from the event.keyCode object, and uses a switch statement to assign a code for each remote control key. The above code declared only key events needed by the category anchor, based on the Hands Frame application design.

The next step is defining how each member list element of the category element handles focus. Assume the next situation for this explanation.

- The application has been running and the category anchor is focused.
- The category anchor is focused, and its first member element is selected.
- The member elements do not have an anchor.

To implement focus handling of a selected member element, the new index concept needs to be introduced. An index variable defines which <li> member element is currently selected. The index value changes with the up and down directional keys input, while the category anchor is focused. This index value is also used to apply different styles to the selected list member element.

Pressing the right directional key while the category anchor is focused moves the focus to the content scene for the current category selection. Pressing the up directional key that generally selects the above list member does nothing if the currently selected element is the first <li> element. This applies to the last <li> element on the opposite side.

The "selected" concept is introduced to distinguish the anchorless list elements that cannot be focused in the same way. This new index concept is useful to implement the focus without using anchors.

See the next example for the index system that implements the focus scenario for the category element's member list items. The example only handles the up and down directional keys at this point.

```
var index = 0;

Main.category.keyDown = function()
{
    var keyCode = event.keyCode;

    switch(keyCode)
    {
        case tvKey.KEY_RETURN:
            widgetAPI.sendReturnEvent();
            break;
        case tvKey.KEY_RIGHT:
            break;
        case tvKey.KEY_UP:
            Main.category.li.eq(index).removeClass('focus');
            Main.category.li.eq(--index).addClass('focus');
            break;
        case tvKey.KEY_DOWN:
            Main.category.li.eq(index).removeClass('focus');
            Main.category.li.eq(++index).addClass('focus');
            break;
        case tvKey.KEY_INFO :
            break;
        default:
            alert("Unhandled key");
            break;
    }
};
```

The category list does not have any target on its left side. Therefore, it should
ignore the left directional key input while moving the focus to the content anchor
of the selected menu item (in the section area) if there is a right directional key
input. As explained in chapter 5 while covering the focus, jQuery's addClass()
and removeClass() are used to assign a distinct style to the newly focused
element.

Completed source code for the event handling for the category scene is shown below, with some additional code for exception handling.

```javascript
Main.category.keyDown = function()
{
    var keyCode = event.keyCode;

    switch(keyCode)
    {
        case tvKey.KEY_RETURN:
            widgetAPI.sendReturnEvent();
            break;
        case tvKey.KEY_RIGHT:
            break;
        case tvKey.KEY_UP:
            if(index > 0){
                Main.category.li.eq(index).removeClass('focus');
                Main.category.li.eq(--index).addClass('focus');
            }
            break;
        case tvKey.KEY_DOWN:
            if(index < Main.category.li.size() - 1){
                Main.category.li.eq(index).removeClass('focus');
                Main.category.li.eq(++index).addClass('focus');
            }
            break;
        case tvKey.KEY_INFO :
            break;
        default:
            alert("Unhandled key");
            break;
    }
};
```

Contents Pane

In a standard web page, a menu selection causes a contents pane to load a page for the selected menu. The same user interface also needs to be provided by the Hands Frame applications.

Let's first add <div> elements for the content scenes in the index.html, as shown below.

```
<div id="scene_main" >
    <div id="header"></div>
    <div id="category">
        <ul>
            <li class="work">Work</li>
            <li class="people">People</li>
            <li class="dream">Dream</li>
        </ul>
    </div>
    <div id="content">
        <div class="work">Work</div>
        <div class="people">People</div>
        <div class="dream">Dream</div>
    </div>
</div>

<a href="javascript:void(0);" id="anchor_category" onkeydown="Main.category.
keyDown();"></a>
<a href="javascript:void(0);" id="anchor_content" onkeydown="Main.content.
keyDown();"></a>
```

Each of the content elements is hidden and shown when the corresponding category is selected. Consider these scenes as subscreen layers. Each of the content elements plays a VOD file. See below for styles for the content elements.

```
#content{
    float: right;
    position: absolute;
```

```
        left: 313px;
        top: 92px;
        width: 900px;
    }


    #content  > div{
        width: 100%;
        display: none;
    }
```

Note that the #content > div element has a "display: none;" property setting. As screen layers, all content scenes must be hidden except the one that is currently focused. See the next code for the implementation.

The next function handles the content elements.

```
Main.loadContent = function(){
    jQuery('#content').find('div').hide();
    jQuery('#content').find('div').eq(index).show();
};
```

The above function can be called within event-handling code blocks for the up and down keys to show the hidden content scene for the selected category item on the contents pane. Using the categories pane's list to control what's displayed in the contents pane is core logic of the reference application.

```
Main.category.keyDown = function()
{
    var keyCode = event.keyCode;

    switch(keyCode)
    {
        case tvKey.KEY_RETURN:
            widgetAPI.sendReturnEvent();
            break;
```

```
        case tvKey.KEY_RIGHT:
            break;
        case tvKey.KEY_UP:
            if(index > 0){
                Main.category.li.eq(index).removeClass('focus');
                Main.category.li.eq(--index).addClass('focus');
                Main.loadContent();
            }
            break;
        case tvKey.KEY_DOWN:
            if(index < Main.category.li.size() - 1){
                Main.category.li.eq(index).removeClass('focus');
                Main.category.li.eq(++index).addClass('focus');
                Main.loadContent();
            }
            break;
        case tvKey.KEY_INFO :
            break;
        default:
            alert("Unhandled key");
            break;
    }
};
```

After a content scene is displayed in the contents pane, the next step is implementing handing over the focus to the currently displayed content scene. Also, the newly focused content scene needs to be marked. In this example, its font color will be changed to red using the next style element.

```
#content.focus  > div{
    color: red;
}
```

While the categories anchor is focused, pressing the right directional key transfers the focus to the contents pane. See the following keyDown() function for the implementation within the case block tvKey.KEY_RIGHT:

```javascript
Main.category.keyDown = function()
{
    var keyCode = event.keyCode;

    switch(keyCode)
    {
        case tvKey.KEY_RETURN:
            widgetAPI.sendReturnEvent();
            break;
        case tvKey.KEY_RIGHT:
            Main.content.anchor.focus();
            Main.category.elem.removeClass('focus');
            Main.content.elem.addClass('focus');
            break;
        case tvKey.KEY_UP:
            if(index > 0){
                Main.category.li.eq(index).removeClass('focus');
                Main.category.li.eq(--index).addClass('focus');
                Main.loadContent();
            }
            break;
        case tvKey.KEY_DOWN:
            if(index < Main.category.li.size() - 1){
                Main.category.li.eq(index).removeClass('focus');
                Main.category.li.eq(++index).addClass('focus');
                Main.loadContent();
            }
            break;
        case tvKey.KEY_INFO :
            break;
        default:
            alert("Unhandled key");
            break;
    }
};
```

The above block transfers the focus to the contents pane's anchor, and marks the newly focused content scene by changing its font color to red. The next code shows how to return the focus back to the category item when the left directional key is pressed.

```
Main.content.keyDown = function()
{
    var keyCode = event.keyCode;

    switch(keyCode)
    {
        case tvKey.KEY_RETURN:
        case tvKey.KEY_PANEL_RETURN:
            widgetAPI.sendReturnEvent();
            break;
        case tvKey.KEY_LEFT:
            Main.category.anchor.focus();
            Main.content.elem.removeClass('focus');
            Main.category.elem.addClass('focus');
            break;
        case tvKey.KEY_RIGHT:
            break;
        case tvKey.KEY_UP:
            break;
        case tvKey.KEY_DOWN:
            break;
        case tvKey.KEY_ENTER:
        case tvKey.KEY_PANEL_ENTER:
            break;
        default:
            break;
    }
};
```

The code uses jQuery's addClass() and removeClass() to change styles of focused or unfocused elements to inform users of the current focus. This concludes the

Hands Frame application's basic navigation logic for layout, screen changing, and basic focus handling.

Check the addendum for the complete source code of the application to see how the example codes are integrated.

VOD Player

As of now, a newly shown and focused content scene only changes its font color to red to indicate the change. But the original design of the Hands Frame application also includes playing a VOD file.

The Samsung SmartTV's internal AVPlayer module will be used to display the VOD file. Let's jump into actually adding the AVPlayer library within this application, since the library was already well discussed in chapter 7, AV Player.

A container <div> element will be used to contain the player module.

```
<!-- player container -->
<div id="player_container"></div>
```

The player container's major functions are bringing the movie-playing screen to the front of the rest of the application, and providing an easy access point to control the screen properties. See the following code for styles for the player container.

```
#player_container {
    position: absolute;
    width: 1280px;
    height: 720px;
    opacity: 0;
    left: 0;
    top: 0;
}
```

```css
#player_container.show {
    opacity: 1;
}
```

Next, declare the Web API library, which includes the AV Player within the index.html file. Then declare an anchor for the player.

```html
<script type="text/javascript" language="javascript" src="$MANAGER_WIDGET/
Common/webapi/1.0/webapis.js"></script>

<a href="javascript:void(0);" id="anchor_player" onkeydown="Main.player.
keyDown();"></a>
```

The declared anchor_player anchor is focused and receives remote control key events while a VOD file is playing. For example, the remote control play or stop key events can be implemented to play or stop the VOD playing. See the next code for the handler function that is used by the anchor_player.

```javascript
Main.player.keyDown = function()
{
    var keyCode = event.keyCode;
    switch(keyCode)
    {
        case tvKey.KEY_RETURN:
            event.preventDefault();
            break;
        case tvKey.KEY_PLAY:
            break;
        case tvKey.KEY_STOP:
            break;
        default:
            break;
    }
};
```

Note that event.preventDefault() was inserted in the tv.KEY_RETURN: case block to prevent the application from terminating when the return or exit key is pressed. This topic will be discussed in the later Exception Handling chapter in more detail.

Player Object

The player module can be included either in an existing scene or in an exclusive VOD-playing-only scene, with its own JavaScript file. The exclusive scene method is more versatile and better suited for a large application with full screen / windowed mode transition, a remote information window, subtitles, and other complex player event handling.

However, the Hands Frame application only needs simple play and stop functions. The next example will use the main screen layer to include the player module.

```
// path for a movie file
var URL = 'C://Users/Administrator/Videos/1_1.mp4';

var Player = {
    init : function(){
        try{
            var playerInstance = deviceapis.avplay;
            playerInstance.getAVPlay(Player.onAVPlayObtained, Player.
onGetAVPlayError);

        }catch(e){
            alert('######getAVplay Exception :[' +e.code + '] ' +
e.message);
        }
    },
    onAVPlayObtained : function(avplay){
        // callback function for initializing the AVPlayer module
        Main.AVPlayer = avplay;
        Main.AVPlayer.init({containerID : 'player_container', displayRect:
{
            top: 0,
```

```
                    left: 0,
                    width: 1280,
                    height: 720
            }, autoRatio: true });
    },
    onGetAVPlayError : function(){
        // error handling function for initializing the AVPlayer module
        alert('######onGetAVPlayError: ' + error.message);
    },
    onError : function(){
        alert('######onError: ');
    },
    onSuccess : function(){
        alert('######onSuccess: ');
    },
    play: function() {
        try{
            jQuery('#player_container').addClass('show');
            Main.AVPlayer.open(URL);
            Main.AVPlayer.play(Player.onSuccess, Player.onError);

        }catch(e){
            alert(e.message);
        }
    },
    stop: function() {
        jQuery('#player_container').removeClass('show');
        Main.AVPlayer.stop();
    }
};
```

See the source code where Main.AVPlayer.init() receives a callback parameter to initialize the player module. This allows binding the player module to the previously declared player container. Except that the API is bound under the player object, it was implemented exactly as shown in chapter 7, AV Player. See the previous chapter for details. The player is implemented with only play and stop capabilities.

Only one static file link was entered as the VOD source. However, an array of URLs was used in the attached final source code for the Hands Frame – Basic so that it can play a different VOD for each focused menu item.

The next function plays the VOD file.

```
Player.play();
```

Pause and resume capabilities are not too difficult to add under the preceding player object. However, this example will include play and stop capabilities only. See the next example for an event-handling function that only handles those two.

```
Main.player.keyDown = function()
{
    var keyCode = event.keyCode;

    switch(keyCode)
    {
        case tvKey.KEY_RETURN:
            event.preventDefault();
            Player.stop();
            Main.content.anchor.focus();
            break;
        case tvKey.KEY_PLAY:
            Player.play();
            break;
        case tvKey.KEY_STOP:
            Player.stop();
            Main.content.anchor.focus();
            break;
        default:
            break;
    }
};
```

Note that the preceding code returns the focus to anchor_content after the player stops. This returns control of the application to the contents pane, which called the player module. Review chapter 7, AV Player, for the details and other useful tips.

This concludes most of the developing Hands Frame – Basic application. See the complete source code in the addendum for the information scene and dynamic URL that were not covered in this chapter.

Summary

The Hands Frame is a simple reference application that helps in understanding basics of Samsung SmartTV application development, including scenes-based focus handling and movie player. This application provides reference materials on ideas, culture, and contact information of the author of this book, Handstudio company. See the addendum for the complete source code.

The following link provides additional information about the sample application.

▶ Download URL: https://bitbucket.org/handstudio/handsframe/

09

Server-Side Data Processing

The Samsung SmartTV does not support server-side services, including database servers, or a standard connectivity model such as ODBC. Instead, Ajax-type server-side data handling is common using XML or the JSON API.

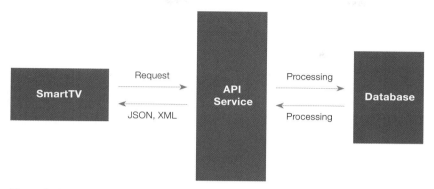

Figure 9-1. The Samsung SmartTV and Server-Side Data Request

Chapter 9 will cover data exchanging between a Samsung SmartTV and a server, including necessary API design, API data processing, and optimizing server-side requests.

API Design

The design of an application depends on how efficiently its data server responds to API requests on necessary data for the application. A well-designed application development project can significantly reduce its development schedule. For efficient API data exchanges, it is vital for a developer to familiarize oneself with the server API, and actively consult with the data provider.

Chapter 9 will use the previously developed Hands Frame application to explain the API design practice.

Designing API for a VOD Gallery

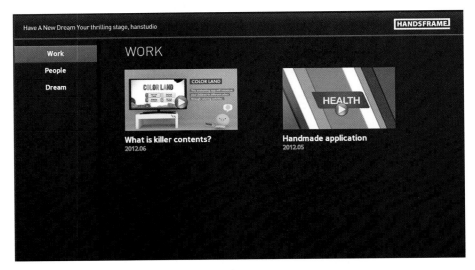

Figure 9-2. An Example VOD Gallery Application

The application shown in Figure 9-2 has a static menu list of titles in the left pane, and a focused menu item shows a list of VOD files for the item. To display meta information for the VOD files as shown above, an API concept can be designed as shown below.

Request Parameters

Parameter	Type	Description
titleId	String	Unique ID for the VOD

Table 9-1. Request Parameters for the VOD Gallery

Response Data Structure

Field Name	Type	Description
titleId	String	Unique ID for the VOD
title	String	Title of the VOD

Field Name	Type	Description
date	String	Registered date for the VOD
thumbnail	String	Thumbnail address for the VOD
vodURL	String	Location for the VOD
Description	Text	Description for the VOD
State	Boolean	If the VOD is currently active

Table 9-2. Data Structure of the VOD Gallery Response

The API structure is similar to a common bulletin board service's data structure. A titleid (unique ID for each VOD title) is used as the key value in a POST or GET request, and for receiving the corresponding data from the server.

XML Type Response with the Data Structure

An XML-type API Response with the above data structure is shown in the following example.

```
<vod>
    <titleId>001</titleId>
    <title>Hello! This is your SmartTV</title>
    <date>2013-01-23</date>
    <thumbnail><![CDATA[http://thumbnails.com/thumbnail.jpg]]></thumbnail>
    <vodURL><![CDATA[http://vod.com/vod.mp4]]></vodURL>
    <description>
    A SmartTV, sometimes referred to as a connected TV or hybrid TV (not
to be confused with IPTV, Internet TV, or Web TV), describes a trend of
integration of the Internet and Web 2.0 features into television sets and
set-top boxes.
    </description>
    <state>true</state>
</vod>
```

JSON Type Response with the Data Structure

A JSON type API Response with the above data structure is shown in the following example.

```
{
    "titleId":
    "001",
    "title": "Hello! This is your SmartTV",
    "date": "2013-01-23",
    "thumbnail": "http://thumbnails.com/thumbnail.jpg",
    "vodURL": "http://vod.com/vod.mp4",
     "description": "A SmartTV, sometimes referred to as a connected TV or
hybrid TV (not to be confused with IPTV, Internet TV, or Web TV), describes
a trend of integration of the Internet and Web 2.0 features into television
sets and set-top boxes",
    "state": "true"
}
```

XML vs. JSON

It was already mentioned that most API services in the SmartTV are provided in either the XML or the JSON format, and occasionally in a plain-text format. Many developers prefer the JSON type. But that does not mean JSON is superior to other types. Each environment calls a different response type for more efficient processing. The JSON format is optimized for the web platform, easy to use, light-weight, and most of all, fits the object-oriented JavaScript model. On the other hand, the XML format is supported by many platforms, easily readable, and supplied with a wealth of reference information.

Type	JSON	XML
Pros	• Concise with only necessary data • Optimized for JavaScript data handling • Easy to use	• Easy to write • Easy to read • Well referenced
Cons	• Not as easy as XML to read • Not suitable for receiving large data	• Bloated file size • Hard to parse data

Table 9-3. JSON vs. XML

Efficient API Handling and Conclusion

A large portion of API design is up to the API provider's system environment. An application developer's API design is limited by available options by the API provider. Some API providers have severely limited options or even fixed-API structure only, rendering concept of the API design meaningless.

Even so, creating and managing an API structure table, as shown previously, can still save a huge amount of unnecessary communication with the service company. The table can be used during the entire development and debugging. It can also be shared with non-programmers: producers, designers, and clients—and allow them to quickly check if a desired function can be implemented.

API Processing

A data-request API is commonly processed in the following order.

1. Receive an Ajax request.
2. Obtain the requested data and format it as a predefined return-object variable.
3. Return the variable through a DOM exchange.

A JavaScript library is often used to simplify the preceding Ajax request and DOM exchange. The jQuery (http://jquery.com/) library is used in this book.

Ajax Request

First, an Ajax request is implemented using the jQuery library.

```
jQuery.ajax(url, {
    type : 'GET',
    dataType : "xml",
    data: param,
    timeout: 5000,
```

```
    success: function(res, status, xhr) {
        alert('res :' + res);
        callback && callback(res);
    },
    error : function(xhr, status, error) {
        alert('error! : [Featured] ajax request URL : ' + url);
    },
    complete : function() {
        alert('Complete! : [Featured] ajax request URL : ' + url);
    }
});
```

The preceding example has only the bare minimum options. It configures URL for the API request to be sent, GET or POST option, response API type, and callback functions for success/error/complete cases. See the following code for packaging the request as a usable component.

```
var $request = function(url, param, callback) {
    jQuery.ajax(url, {
        type : 'GET',
        dataType : "xml",
        data: param,
        timeout: 5000,
        success: function(res, status, xhr) {
            alert('res :' + res);
            callback && callback(res);
        },
        error : function(xhr, status, error) {
            alert('error! : [Featured] ajax request URL : ' + url);
        },
        complete : function() {
            alert('Complete! : [Featured] ajax request URL : ' + url);
        }
    });
};
```

The $request() function can be called with parameters to make an Ajax request for an XML type data. The SmartTV does not have an exclusive Ajax format. Most programming practices, including native JavaScript and jQuery, can also be used for a SmartTV application.

Formatting Response Data

A SmartTV application generally has several element options, such as a menu, VOD playback, and text documents. A common API also has various options. It can have either JSON or XML data type. It can also have a response structure such as List, Map, or String. It is vital to format a response into a usable variable through a well-designed API request. See the following XML document.

```xml
<?xml version="1.0" encoding="UTF-8"?>
<API>
    <item>
        <itemId>001</itemId>
        <itemName>The 2011 SmartTV</itemName>
        <itemState>false</itemState>
    </item>
    <item>
        <itemId>002</itemId>
        <itemName>The 2012 SmartTV</itemName>
        <itemState>false</itemState>
    </item>
    <item>
        <itemId>003</itemId>
        <itemName>The 2013 SmartTV</itemName>
        <itemState>true</itemState>
    </item>

</API>
```

Include a callback function, success(), in the Ajax request, to reformat the preceding XML data.

```
jQuery.ajax(url, {
    type : 'GET',
    dataType : "xml",
    success: function(res) {
        var result = jQuery(res).find('API > item');
    }
});
```

The success() callback function uses jQuery find() to access the XML element. Then it stores a member array "item" from the root element "API" into the variable result.

```
jQuery.isArray(result);    // true
```

The jQuery isArray() can be used to confirm that the result is an array type variable. Let's see another example.

```
{
    "API": {
        "item": [
            {
                "itemId": "001",
                "itemName": "2011SmartTV",
                "itemState": "false"
            },
            {
                "itemId": "002",
                "itemName": "2012 SmartTV",
                "itemState": "false"
            },
            {
                "itemId": "003",
                "itemName": "2013 SmartTV",
```

```
        "itemState": "true"
      }
    ]
  }
}
```

The preceding source code converts an XML result into a JSON type data.

jQuery ajax() can be supplied with different parameter values to format the response data.

```
jQuery.ajax(url, {
    type : 'GET',
    dataType : "json",
    success: function(res) {
        var result = res.API.item;
    }
});
```

Optimizing API Requests

The Ajax request is a memory-intensive JavaScript process. Simultaneous Ajax requests from an application can cause device memory shortage that can result in a failed request or even halt the application.

Therefore, a developer needs to consider the preceding potential issue and be prepared for simultaneous multiple requests.

Minimize Number of API Requests

In a general web bulletin board, selecting a list item causes the application to make a new request for detailed data of the selected item using its key code. However, allowing this habit in the SmartTV application development and making a new request each time a scene changes may cause memory shortage. It is better to make a small number of comprehensive requests. See the following code for the API.

```xml
<?xml version="1.0" encoding="UTF-8"?>
<API>
    <item>
        <itemId>001</itemId>
        <itemName>The 2011 SmartTV</itemName>
    </item>
    <item>
        <itemId>002</itemId>
        <itemName>The 2012 SmartTV</itemName>
    </item>
    <item>
        <itemId>003</itemId>
        <itemName>The 2013 SmartTV</itemName>
    </item>

</API>
```

The preceding API requests a list of items. Each item's itemId key element is then used to make the next API request for an item's detailed information.

```xml
<?xml version="1.0" encoding="UTF-8"?>
<API>
    <item>
        <itemId>001</itemId>
        <itemName>The 2011 SmartTV</itemName>
        <itemState>false</itemState>
        <itemDate>2013-01-31</itemState>
        <itemTitle>false</itemState>
        <itemContent>Hello World</itemState>
    </item>
</API>
```

The preceding pattern is commonly used in standard web bulletin board development. Data requests completely rely on API design. And the preceding API design makes multiple API requests unavoidable. However, the next API design allows a single request to handle the preceding data access.

```xml
<?xml version="1.0" encoding="UTF-8"?>
<API>
    <item>
        <itemId>001</itemId>
        <itemName>The 2011 SmartTV</itemName>
        <itemState>false</itemState>
        <itemDate>2013-01-31</itemState>
        <itemTitle>false</itemState>
        <itemContent>Hello World</itemState>
    </item>
    <item>
        <itemId>002</itemId>
        <itemName>The 2012 SmartTV</itemName>
        <itemState>false</itemState>
        <itemDate>2013-01-31</itemState>
        <itemTitle>false</itemState>
        <itemContent>false</itemState>
    </item>
    <item>
        <itemId>003</itemId>
        <itemName>The 2013 SmartTV</itemName>
        <itemState>true</itemState>
        <itemDate>2013-01-31</itemState>
        <itemTitle>false</itemState>
        <itemContent>false</itemState>
    </item>
</API>
```

The first distributed API requests may help neat code management. But the preceding single request method is necessary for the application performance gain. The received response value can be stored within a DOM element, a Java

Bean type object variable, or as an internal SmartTV file using the File API. The following code demonstrates storing response data in a DOM element.

```
jQuery.ajax(url, {
    type : 'GET',
    dataType : "json",
    success: function(res) {
        var result = jQuery(res).find('API > item');
        jQuery('#model').eq(1).attr('itemDate', result[1].find('> itemDate').
text());
    }
});
```

Cache Optimization

Another technique of optimizing the API requests is using cache, which stores a result in a variable using a unique ID, and reuses the stored value the next time the same data is needed, instead of making a new request. This is highly useful in an application with frequent API requests. The following code declares a variable to store the results.

```
var cache = {};    // global variable
```

Then the Ajax result is paired with a unique ID and stored as a member property of the cache variable.

```
jQuery.ajax(url, {
    type : 'GET',
    dataType : "json",
    success: function(res) {
        var result = jQuery(res);
        cache['0011AA'] = result;    // unique id = 0011AA
    }
});
```

The result variable holding the API response is stored under the cache variable. If another request for the same data is received, then the code uses the cached data without making a new server API request.

```
if (!cache['0011AA']) {
    jQuery.ajax(url, {
        type : 'GET',
        dataType : "json",
        success: function(res) {
            var result = jQuery(res);
            cache['0011AA'] = result;    // unique id = 0011AA
            callback(cache['0011AA']);
        }
    });
} else {
    callback(cache['0011AA']);
}
```

While the preceding code defines a static random ID, an ID management system needs to be implemented in a real application.

Cache optimization is a highly efficient technique that can eliminate many requests. However, it has its own limit on handling frequently updated data, since it reuses already stored data.

Summary

The Ajax request is the preferred method to access server-side data in a SmartTV application. The response data needs to be in an API structure such as XML or JSON. The resulting data needs to be formatted to suit the situation. The process also needs to be memory optimized to handle limited memory capacity of SmartTV devices.

10

IME

A SmartTV application often includes a search or login feature to meet its service purpose. The Samsung SmartTV provides the IME module to collect user data input. The IME can be accessed by using a remote controller, through a virtual keyboard, as shown below.

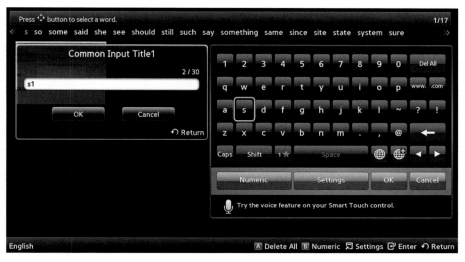

Figure 10-1. Text Input Using the IME

Using IME

Initialization

The first step in using an IME is adding an <input> element on the HTML page.

```
<input id="ime_test" type="text" size="10" maxlength="256" height="30" />
```

The preceding <input> element displays the user IME input, while also helping in creating an IME object and handling the focus. Make sure to assign a maxlength value to avoid user confusion and IME system errors resulting from endless typing. The maxlength property can have a maximum value of 256 characters.

In addition to the <input> element, the Common Module API needs to be loaded since it includes the IME module. This allows the IME to be called.

```
<!-- IME module -->
    <script type="text/javascript" language="javascript" src="$MANAGER_WIDGET/
Common/IME_XT9/ime.js"></script>
    <script type="text/javascript" language="javascript" src="$MANAGER_WIDGET/
Common/IME_XT9/inputCommon/ime_input.js"></script>
```

The declared Common Module API can be used to receive an IME instance to create an IME object. An <input> element's ID must be immediately entered into the newly created object's inputboxID member variable.

```
// create an IME object
// set InputBox ID in the IME object
oIME = new IMEShell_Common();
oIME.inputboxID = "ime_test";
```

Assuming a correct inputboxID value is entered, the IME module will be called when the input box is selected. Once the IME module is called, it will take care of the user remote control input process on its own.

onKeyPressFunc( ) Callback Function

The onKeyPressFunc() is vital for using the IME module.

```
// this callback function handles key press events
// that cause the IME module to exit.
oIME.onKeyPressFunc = function(keyCode) {
    switch(keyCode)
    {
        case tvKey.KEY_RETURN:
            break;
        case tvKey.KEY_EXIT:
            break;
        case tvKey.KEY_ENTER:
            break;
    }
};
```

The onKeyPressFunc() is very important because it defines how the application reacts when IME user input is complete. This function can modify the input data and allocate it to necessary UI components.

The onKeyPressFunc() always runs when the IME module exits, which is caused by pressing the remote control exit or return key, or by selecting OK or the return key on the virtual keyboard.

The following custom function calls the IME module with its internally defined onKeyPressFunc().

```
var focusIME = function() {
    oIME = new IMEShell_Common();
    oIME.inputboxID = "ime_test";
    oIME.onKeyPressFunc = function(keyCode) {
        switch(keyCode)
        {
```

```
        case tvKey.KEY_RETURN:
            break;
        case tvKey.KEY_EXIT:
            break;
        case tvKey.KEY_ENTER:
            break;
        }
    };


    jQuery('#ime_test').focus();
    oIME.onShow();
};
```

IME Member Functions

The following member functions are also frequently used while using the IME module.

onClose( ) Function	
Closes the IME	
Grammar	onClose()
Usage	imeBox.onClose();

Table 10-1. IME.onClose()

inputTitle( ) Function	
Sets title for the IME module's pop-up window (not supported in 2013 models)	
Grammar	inputTitle = "";
Usage	imeBox.inputTitle = "Common Input Title1";

Table 10-2. IME.inputTitle()

onCompleteFunc Property	
Sets a callback function to be called when data auto-completion is activated	
Grammar	`onCompleteFunc = callback function`

Usage	`imeBox.onCompleteFunc = onCompleteText;`
	`function onCompleteText(arg) {`
	    `alert("onCompleteText ===================: " + arg);`
	`}`

Table 10-3. IME.onCompleteFunc

showAutoCompletePopup( ) Function	
Displays the auto-completed text	
Grammar	`showAutoCompletePopup(items)`

Usage	`var dataObj ={`
	        `request : "w",   // IME input text`
	        `items : ["www.naver.com","www.google.com","www.baykoreans.net","www.`
	    `yahoo.co.kr","www.yesfile.com","www.itemmania.com"]`
	        `// Data will be shown in the list`
	    `};`

Table 10-4. IME.showAutoCompletePopup()

The SDF guides use the onClose function to manually close any open IME module.

12 Keys and QWERTY Keyboards

12 Keys Type

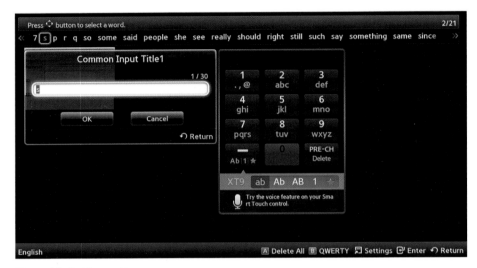

Figure 10-2. 12 Keys Type

The 12 Keys keyboard is similar to the 9 numeric keys on a SmartTV remote controller. Only the input element can be focused in this IME type, which will display a bound value or generate an even value whenever one of the 12 keys is pressed. The lower-left "-" key will switch the keyboard type.

QWERTY Type

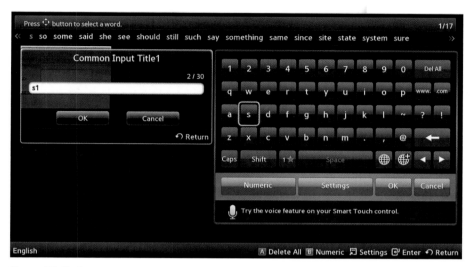

Figure 10-3. QWERTY Type

Figure 10-4. QWERTY Type (2013)

The QWERTY keyboard is similar to a regular computer keyboard. All the virtual keyboard buttons, in addition to the input box, can receive the focus. Use the four directional keys to move the focus to a desired button and press to enter a character.

The 12 Keys and QWERTY keyboards have almost the same programming methods, except some minor differences. The IME module can control both of the keyboards, which can be tested by the Emulator. The last-used keyboard by the user will become the default keyboard in the next IME input. The two keyboards can be switched during an input, with a remote controller.

Summary

The IME module is the most common way to get user input in a SmartTV application. The IME module is matched to an <input> element ID, and requires some exception handling. The SDF provides many member functions and properties to help in using the IME, which can be used to implement advanced functions such as login and keyword searches in a SmartTV application.

11

The Convergence and AllShare Framework

Popularity of smart phones and SmartTVs eventually called need of a convergence framework that supports interaction between different platforms. In addition to the smart phones and SmartTVs, recent cameras and cars are also equipped with smart functions. With the concept of the Samsung Smart Home that combines all smart electronics, the Convergence has become popular. The Samsung SmartTV supports the Convergence API for interacting with other devices and leads this trend.

Introducing the Convergence

What is the Convergence?

In a Samsung SmartTV application, the Convergence means the Convergence App API that supports a Samsung SmartTV application to communicate with other devices and allows them to control the application. The Samsung SmartTV Convergence provides a REST-type interface for this connection. This implementation requires other devices to support HTTP (including UPnP) to connect the application. (The Convergence and the Convergence App API will be used in interchanging matter.)

While there are many devices that can access a Samsung SmartTV application, this book will use an Android Smart Phone to explain the Convergence. This chapter is primarily written for developers experienced in Android programming, but also can be read for a broad conceptual understanding.

The chapter will show two Convergence practices, and how they are implemented in both a SmartTV application and an Android smart phone. Finally, this chapter will introduce the AllShare framework, which provides an easier communication between Samsung devices only.

Please check the SDF (SDF -> Guide - > API -> Convergence App) for APIs that are not covered in this chapter.

See below for recommended system requirements for testing the following examples.

Samsung SmartTV	2012, 2013 models
Android Smart Phone	A Samsung Galaxy model is recommended because it will connect to a Samsung SmartTV app optimized for Samsung devices. Most Samsung Galaxy models can be used.
Network	Connect both the Samsung SmartTV and a smart phone to the same wireless router. Make sure that the smart phone is not using a 3G or LTE mobile network.

Table **11-1.** System Requirements for Testing the Convergence Example

Application Scenario for the Convergence App

This chapter will use the Gingerbread Man, a children's storybook application developed by Handstudio, to demonstrate a Convergence application scenario.

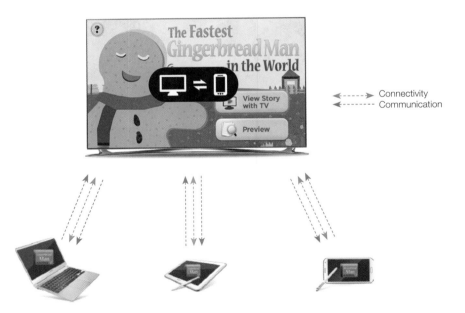

Figure **11-1.** Interaction of a Convergence App – Gingerbread Man

1. Gingerbread Man – a Convergence app – starts on a Samsung SmartTV.

2. A client version of the Gingerbread app starts on a smart phone / tablet / PC, uses UPnP protocol to search a local Samsung SmartTV, and then connects to the running Gingerbread TV application. (Note that the Gingerbread Man application only supports one device connection at a time, but the Samsung SmartTV Convergence platform is capable of supporting up to four simultaneous connections.)

3. Connected devices communicate with each other using the Convergence platform.

Connecting a Mobile Device to a SmartTV

There are two methods for connecting a SmartTV and a mobile device — UPnP and HTTP. The SDF recommends the UPnP method.

UPnP

The UPnP (Universal Plug and Play) method presents a device on a local network so that other devices can sense and connect it without additional configuration. It allows a SmartTV and other local devices to automatically share IP addresses.

HTTP

The HTTP method requires a SmartTV's IP address to be manually entered on a mobile device. This allows more direct and controlled access. Once devices are connected, the JSON format is used to exchange types and messages.

Server-Side (SmartTV) Convergence Application

Loading the Convergence API

See below for concept diagrams of full duplex communication between a mobile client and a SmartTV server.

POST Request

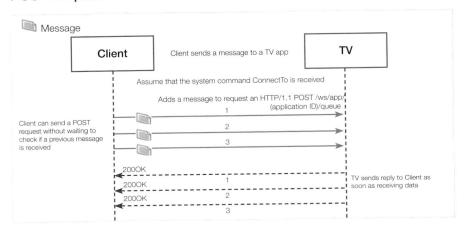

Figure 11-2. Client Sending Message to TV App

GET Request

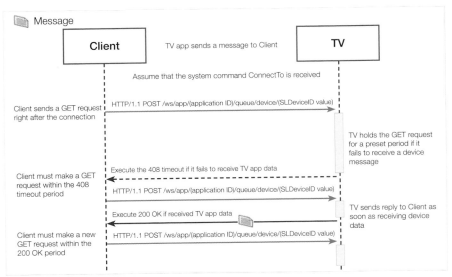

Figure 11-3. TV App Sending Message to Client

In the SmartTV programming, the Web API contains all Convergence functions.

```
<script type="text/javascript" language="javascript" src="$MANAGER_WIDGET/
Common/webapi/1.0/webapis.js"></script>
```

Once the API is declared, all the Web API Convergence member functions and properties can be accessed with JavaScript.

```
this._API = window.webapis.customdevice || {};
```

Declare a variable to initialize a Web API instance to finish preparing to use the Convergence.

Member Functions of the SmartTV Convergence

The SDF provides a guide for member functions of the SmartTV Convergence, for its easier usage. These functions help easy setup and connectivity to other devices without complex network configuration. The following chart lists major Web API functions for the Convergence function.

Function	Description
getCustomDevices(successCallback, errorCallback)	Get an instance of the connected mobile device
registerManagerCallback(callback)	Assign a callback function for connection/ disconnection to a mobile device
registerDeviceCallback(callback)	Assign a callback function for receiving a mobile device message
sendMessage(sMessage)	Sends a message from TV to mobile
broadcastMessage(sMessage)	Sends a message from mobile to TV
multicastMessage(sGroupID,sMessage)	Sends a message to grouped mobile devices

Table 11-2. Samsung SmartTV Convergence App API Functions

The preceding functions take care of all connections between devices. Let's see how they are used in practice.

Communication from Mobile to TV

Function	registerManagerCallback(callback)

Callback	`function(oManagerEvent) {`
	`    alert('UID: ' + oManagerEvent.UID);`
	`    // UID: mobile device ID`
	`    alert('name: ' + oManagerEvent.name);`
	`    // name: mobile device name`
	`    alert('eventType: ' + oManagerEvent.eventType);`
	`    // eventType: mobile status event`
	`    alert('deviceType: ' + oManagerEvent.deviceType);`
	`    // deviceType: mobile device type`
	`}`

Table 11-3. The registerManager Callback Function

The registerManagerCallback() function creates or breaks connection between a Samsung SmartTV and a mobile device. The member callback function receives connectivity information as arguments. The connectivity information includes a mobile status event that tells if the connection was successful. Other callback functions can be assigned for a different status. The connected mobile device's status is stored in the eventType variable.

The next table shows event values generated while connecting or disconnecting to a device. The argument callback function uses this value to see if a device is being connected or disconnected, to decide the next events.

Manager Event	Description
MGR_EVENT_DEV_CONNECT	Mobile disconnect event
MGR_EVENT_DEV_DISCONNECT	Mobile connect event

Table 11-4. Event Values for the registerManager Callback Function

The following example source code uses a registerManager assigned callback function to handle connect or disconnect events of a mobile device to a SmartTV.

```
var Convergence = {
    API: window.webapis.customdevice || {},
    aDevice: [],
    init: function() {
        this.API.registerManagerCallback(Convergence.registerManager);
        this.API.getCustomDevices(Convergence.getCustomDevices);
    },
    registerManager: function(oManagerEvent) {
        var _this = Convergence;

        alert('UID: ' + oManagerEvent.UID);
        // UID: mobile device ID
        alert('name: ' + oManagerEvent.name);
        // name: mobile device name
        alert('eventType: ' + oManagerEvent.eventType);
        // eventType: mobile status event
        alert('deviceType: ' + oManagerEvent.deviceType);
        // deviceType: mobile device type

        switch(oManagerEvent.eventType) {
            case _this.API.MGR_EVENT_DEV_CONNECT:
                alert('MGR_EVENT_DEV_CONNECT');

                _this.API.getCustomDevices(Convergence.getCustomDevices);
                break;
            case _this.API.MGR_EVENT_DEV_DISCONNECT:
                alert('MGR_EVENT_DEV_DISCONNECT');

                _this.API.getCustomDevices(Convergence.getCustomDevices);
                break;
            default:
                alert('EVENT_UNKNOWN');
                break;
        }
    },
Convergence.init();
```

The next getCustomDevices() function receives an instance of the connected device as an array property. The device information can be used to assign different callback functions. It is used to update mobile connectivity information when there is a change in mobile connection.

Function	`getCustomDevices(successCallback, errorCallback)`

Callback	`function(aDevice) {`
	`    for(var i = 0; i < aDevice.length; i++) {`
	`        alert('getUniqueID: ' + aDevice[i].getUniqueID());`
	`        // getUniqueID: mobile device ID`
	`        alert('getName: ' + aDevice[i].getName());`
	`        // getName: mobile device name`
	`        alert('getDeviceID: ' + aDevice[i].getDeviceID());`
	`        // deviceID: mobile device ID`
	`        alert('getType: ' + aDevice[i].getType());`
	`        // getType: mobile device type`
	`    }`
	`}`

Table 11-5. The getCustomDevice( ) Function

The following example uses the getCustomDevice() function.

```
var Convergence = {
    API: window.webapis.customdevice || {},
    aDevice: [],
    init: function() {
        this.API.registerManagerCallback(Convergence.registerManager);
        this.API.getCustomDevices(Convergence.getCustomDevices);
    },
    registerManager: function(oManagerEvent) {
        var _this = Convergence;

        switch(oManagerEvent.eventType) {
            case _this.API.MGR_EVENT_DEV_CONNECT:
                alert('MGR_EVENT_DEV_CONNECT');
```

```
                _this.API.getCustomDevices(Convergence.getCustomDevices);
                break;
            case _this.API.MGR_EVENT_DEV_DISCONNECT:
                alert('MGR_EVENT_DEV_DISCONNECT');
                _this.API.getCustomDevices(Convergence.getCustomDevices);
                break;
            default:
                alert('EVENT_UNKNOWN');
                break;
        }
    },
    getCustomDevices: function(aDevice) {
        var _this = Convergence;

        _this.aDevice = aDevice;
        alert('aDevice.length: ' + aDevice.length);
        for(var i = 0; i < aDevice.length; i++) {
            var sID = aDevice[i].getUniqueID();
            alert('getUniqueID: ' + aDevice[i].getUniqueID());
            // getUniqueID: mobile device ID
            alert('getName: ' + aDevice[i].getName());
            // getName: mobile device name
            alert('getDeviceID: ' + aDevice[i].getDeviceID());
            // deviceID: mobile device ID
            alert('getType: ' + aDevice[i].getType());
            // getType: mobile device type

            aDevice[i].registerDeviceCallback(function(oDeviceInfo) {
                _this.registerDevice(sID, oDeviceInfo);
            });
        }
    }
};
Convergence.init();
```

The next registerDeviceCallback() function receives an instance of the connected mobile device and uses it to set events for the assigned callback function. The infoType property holds status information of the mobile instance. Table 11-7 lists possible event values of the infoType property. This function is used to assign behavior according to a message from a mobile device.

Function	registerDeviceCallback(callback)

Callback	```function(oDeviceInfo) {
	    alert('infoType: ' + oDeviceInfo.infoType);
	    // infoType: mobile status information
	    alert('data: ' + oDeviceInfo.data);
	    // data: data received from a mobile device
	}```

Table 11-6. The registerDeviceCallback() Function

Device Event	Description
DEV_EVENT_MESSAGE_RECEIVED	Event for receiving a message
DEV_EVENT_JOINED_GROUP	Event for joining a mobile device to the group
DEV_EVENT_LEFT_GROUP	Event for removing a mobile device from the group

Table 11-7. Events List for the registerDevice Callback Function

The next example uses the registerDeviceCallback() function.

```
var Convergence = {
    API: window.webapis.customdevice || {},
    aDevice: [],
    init: function() {
        this.API.registerManagerCallback(Convergence.registerManager);
        this.API.getCustomDevices(Convergence.getCustomDevices);
    },
    registerManager: function(oManagerEvent) {
        var _this = Convergence;

        switch(oManagerEvent.eventType) {
            case _this.API.MGR_EVENT_DEV_CONNECT:
```

```
                alert('MGR_EVENT_DEV_CONNECT');

                _this.API.getCustomDevices(Convergence.getCustomDevices);
                break;
            case _this.API.MGR_EVENT_DEV_DISCONNECT:
                alert('MGR_EVENT_DEV_DISCONNECT');

                _this.API.getCustomDevices(Convergence.getCustomDevices);
                break;
            default:
                alert('EVENT_UNKNOWN');
                break;
        }
    },
    getCustomDevices: function(aDevice) {
        var _this = Convergence;

        _this.aDevice = aDevice;
        alert('aDevice.length: ' + aDevice.length);
        for(var i = 0; i < aDevice.length; i++) {
            var sID = aDevice[i].getUniqueID();

            aDevice[i].registerDeviceCallback(function(oDeviceInfo) {
                _this.registerDevice(sID, oDeviceInfo);
            });
        }
    },
    registerDevice: function(sID, oDeviceInfo) {
        var _this = Convergence;

        alert('sID: ' + sID);
        // sID: unique mobile device ID
        alert('infoType: ' + oDeviceInfo.infoType);
        // infoType: mobile device information type
        for(var key in oDeviceInfo.data) {
            alert(key + ' : ' + oDeviceInfo.data[key]);
        }
        // data: data received from the mobile device
```

```
        switch(oDeviceInfo.infoType) {
            case _this.API.DEV_EVENT_MESSAGE_RECEIVED:
                alert('DEV_EVENT_MESSAGE_RECEIVED');
                break;
            case _this.API.DEV_EVENT_JOINED_GROUP:
                alert('DEV_EVENT_JOINED_GROUP');
                break;
            case _this.API.DEV_EVENT_LEFT_GROUP:
                alert('EVENT_DEVICE_LEFT_GROUP');
                break;
        }
    }
};
Convergence.init();
```

File Transfer from Mobile to TV

The Convergence App API can also transfer files, in addition to sending text messages. This allows a mobile device to send an image file to a SmartTV and display it on the TV screen. In this case, the SmartTV application only needs to get the location of the mobile transferred image file and display it on the desired coordinate.

Size	3MB
URL	'http://' + SmartTV IP address + '/ws/app/' + curWidget.id + '/file/' + Image filename;
Example	'http://127.0.0.1/ws/app/ConvergenceTest/file/image.jpg';

Table 11-8. Example of Image File Transfer Format

Maximum file size for the mobile to Samsung SmartTV transfer is 3MB. However, it is recommended to use the smallest possible files to avoid network delay. Note that the transfer cannot replace an existing file. The preceding URL address format is used to display an image file on the SmartTV screen.

Communication from TV to Mobile

A SmartTV can also transfer data to a mobile device. The next member functions enable the data transfer.

Function	sendMessage(sMessage)
Example	oDevice.sendMessage(sMessage)
Purpose	Send a message to a mobile device

Function	broadcastMessage(sMessage)
Example	oDevice.broadcastMessage(sMessage);
Purpose	Send a message to all mobile devices connected to the SmartTV

Function	multicastMessage(sGroupID, sMessage)
Example	oDevice.multicastMessage(sGroupID, sMessage);
Purpose	Send a message to all mobile devices with the same group ID

Table 11-9. Data Transfer Member Functions

Client-Side (a Mobile Device) Convergence Application

Protocol Design

Introduction

A Convergence app functions through a connection between mobile devices and a SmartTV. This calls for a protocol that will connect two different devices. Samsung Electronics' SDF provides the Convergence App API Guide to provide request header and application methods information.

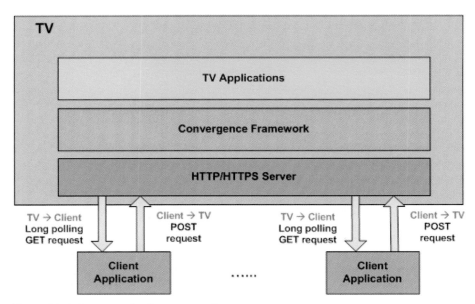

Figure 11 -4. Structure of a Convergence App

Figure 11-4 maps how a Convergence App functions. The design is based on the REST interface and uses a URL format to define all the details for file transfer. This interface is standardized and simpler than the SOAP interface. It allows fast development cycle and fast execution.

The SDF suggested model is using an HTTP protocol-supporting mobile device to discover and connect through the UPnP scan.

This chapter will focus on the mobile device (client) part of the Samsung SmartTV Convergence App API, and explain how to implement connecting, sending a message, sending an image, receiving a message, and disconnecting between an Android-based mobile device and a SmartTV.

Request Header

A mobile device uses the HTTP protocol to send a message to a SmartTV, using the following header information. Some of the header information is mandatory, while some is optional. It is vital to have a clear idea when using the table.

Header	Description	Note
SLDeviceID	Identify a mobile device (client)	Mandatory (except for Get Application info method)
Content-Type	Mark content type	Mandatory for a POST request
ProductID	Identify a smart device	Mandatory for a connection request
VendorID	Identify a smart device manufacturer	Mandatory for a connection request
DeviceName	Display a mobile device name	Mandatory for a connection request
User-Agent	Identify a mobile device type and feature	Mandatory for a connection request
Custom	User-added header	

Table 11-10. Header Information for a Convergence App Request

SLDeviceID

SLDeviceID is a header component that allows a SmartTV application to identify a client device. Usually, a unique device ID (UUID) is used. This component is mandatory for all requests except the Get Application Info method.

Content-Type

This header component indicates the content type in a JSON or XML value. It is mandatory for all POST requests.

ProductID

This header identifies a smart device, and is mandatory for a connection request. Note that the ID must be an exactly eight-letter string that starts with "SMART."

Example: SMARTDev, SMARTtvi, etc.

VendorID

This header identifies the smart device's manufacturer, and is mandatory for a connection request. Note that the ID must also be an exactly eight-letter string.

Example: vendorMe, vendorTV

DeviceName

This header contains the name of the client device, and is mandatory for a connection request. This header can be up to 64 letters.

User-Agent

This header is used to identify type and specification of the client device, and is mandatory for all requests.

Custom

This user-defined header can be added if necessary. It is packaged in a JSON object to be sent.

Response Code

In a Convergence app, a mobile device and a SmartTV communicate using the HTTP protocol. Therefore, its status response code is also the same as the standard HTTP protocol's response code. See the following table for a list of the response codes.

Code		Description
200	OK	SmartTV successfully completed the client request
201	CREATED	Resource was successfully created
204	NO CONTENT	The client request was successfully processed, but the system is out of resources to return
301	MOVED PERMANENTLY	The requested page was permanently relocated
400	BAD REQUEST	SmartTV failed to read the header for incorrect request format (usually for wrong URL, header, or parameters)
401	UNAUTHORIZED	Requires authentication
404	NOT FOUND	Cannot find the requested resource (generated when non-existing resource was requested)
405	METHOD NOT ALLOWED	Cannot execute the requested method
408	REQUEST TIMEOUT	SmartTV failed to process within the request time limit
409	CONFLICT	Conflict while processing the request
413	REQUEST ENTITY TOO LARGE	The uploaded file is over the size limit (Samsung SmartTV has 3MB upload limit)
500	INTERNAL SERVER ERROR	Error while processing the request
503	SERVICE UNAVAILABLE	Maximum allowed devices are already connected (Samsung SmartTV can connect to up to 4 devices)

Table 11-11. Response Code for the Convergence App

Main Methods

Since a Convergence app's main functions are handled through message exchanges between two devices, Connect, Send Message, Send Image, Retrieve Message, and Disconnect are the most frequently used methods. Descriptions and examples of the five major methods follow.

Connect

The Connect method connects a mobile device to a SmartTV. Keyword connect is used for this request. SLDeviceID, VendorID, and ProductID header components are mandatory.

Request Type	POST
URI	/ws/app/(ApplicationID)/connect
Return Value:	**Response Code** 200, 403, 404
Example	(Request) POST /ws/app/(ApplicationID)/connect HTTP/1.1 Accept: */* Accept-Language: en-us SLDeviceID: 12345 VendorID: VenderMe DeviceName: IE-Client ProductID: SMARTDev Accept-Encoding: gzip, deflate User-Agent: Android-Phone Host: 127.0.0.1:8008 Content-Length: 0 Connection: Keep-Alive (Response) HTTP/1.1 200 OK Content-Length: 0 Date: Mon, 14 Jan 2013 2:22 PM Server: lighttpd/1.4.28

Table 11-12. Convergence App Connect Request Header

Send Message

This method adds a message to a SmartTV's message queue. The message body can be transmitted in JSON format. See the following table's (body) label for the JSON-formatted message with type and value pairs.

Request Type	POST
URI	/ws/app/(ApplicationID)/queue
Return Value	Response Code 200

| Example | ```
(Request)
POST /ws/app/(ApplicationID)/queue     HTTP/1.1
Accept: */*
Accept-Language: en-us
SLDeviceID: 12345
Content-Type: application/json
User-Agent: Android-Phone
Host: 127.0.0.1:8008
Content-Length: 56
(Body) {"type":"touchMove","coordinates":{"x":"343","y":"252"}}

(Response)
HTTP/1.1 200 OK
Content-Length: 0
Date: Mon, 14 Jan 2013 2:22 PM
Server: lighttpd/1.4.28
``` |

Table 11-13. Convergence App Send Message Request Header

Send Image

The Send Image request uses the same queue keyword as the Send Message request. Therefore, its header components are also very similar. Instead of the JSON object, this request includes the filename for the image to send.

Request Type	POST
URI	/ws/app/(ApplicationID)/queue
Return Value	Response Code 200
| Example | ```
(Request)
POST /ws/app/(ApplicationID)/queue     HTTP/1.1
User-Agent: Android-Phone
Host: 192.168.1.5
Accept: */*
SLDeviceID: 12345
Content-Length: 13774
Expect: 100-continue;
``` |

Example	Content-Type: multipart/form-data; Content-Type: form-data; name="message"; (Body) {"type":"upload_image","filename": "123.jpg"} (Response) HTTP/1.1 200 OK Content-Length: 0 Date: Mon, 14 Jul 2013 2:34 PM Server: lighttpd/1.4.28

Table 11-14. Convergence App Send Image Request Header

Retrieve Message

This method checks if the SmartTV's message queue has any message to be sent to the mobile device. If there is a message, it will be JSON formatted and returned with a response code. Instead of actually sending a message, a SmartTV simply stores a message in its queue for a mobile device to periodically check and retrieve it.

Request Type	GET
URI	/ws/app/(ApplicationID)/queue/device/(SLDeviceID value)
Return Value	**Response Code** 200, 403, 404, 408 Body (message is included in JSON object)
Example	(Request) GET /ws/app/(ApplicationID)/queue/device/(12345) HTTP/1.1 User-Agent: Android-Phone Host: 127.0.0.1:8008 Accept: */* SLDeviceID:12345 (Response) HTTP/1.1 200 OK Content-type: text/html

| Example | ```
sender: TV
Transfer-Encoding: chunked
Date: Mon, 14 Jul 2013 2:42 PM
Server: lighttpd/1.4.28

(Body) {"type":"echo","coordinates":{"x":"343","y":"252"}}
``` |

Table 11-15. Convergence App Retrieve Message Request Header

Disconnect

The Disconnect method is sent by the mobile device (client) to be disconnected from the SmartTV (server.) The method only works when the two devices are already connected. Otherwise, the 404 response code will be returned.

Request Type	POST
URI	/ws/app/(ApplicationID)/disconnect
Return Value	Response Code 200, 404
| Example | ```
(Request)
POST /ws/app/(ApplicationID)/disconnect    HTTP/1.1
Accept: */*
Accept-Language: en-us
SLDeviceID: 12345
Accept-Encoding: gzip, deflate
User-Agent: Android-Phone
Host: 127.0.0.1:8008
Content-Length: 0
Connection: Keep-Alive
Pragma: no-cache

(Response)
HTTP/1.1
200 OK
Content-Length : 0
Date : Mon, 14 Jul 2013 2:52 PM
Server : lighttpd/1.4.28
``` |

Table 11-16. Convergence App Disconnect Request Header

Connecting a Device

Now that we have reviewed protocols for the mobile device—SmartTV Convergence app, let's see an example that actually connects the two devices. The SDF provides connect() for making a connecting; disconnect() for disconnecting; queue() for message exchange; info() for receiving TV application information; join() for device grouping; and leave() for device ungrouping.

This chapter will cover the more common connect(), disconnect(), and queue() methods to implement connecting, disconnecting, message exchanging, and image transferring. The following examples are for the Android platform.

Please note that some codes were repeated to demonstrate the preceding functions one at a time. For a production app, please increase the efficiency and readability of the code by modulating those repeated codes into functions. Also, it would be better to have separate implementations for AbstractHttpMessage objects, since the GET method is used for message or application information receiving.

> ► Note: http://TV IP address:port/ws/app/applicationID/method

All convergence app communication is processed in the URL format. As shown above, the URL format needs the TV's IP address, port number, TV Application ID, and the communication method. Note that the mobile device and SmartTV need to be in the same local network, and the port number change depends on the network environment. Also, a production app needs to use a Samsung-issued application ID.

An Internet router is commonly used to develop a convergence app. An Internet router usually assigns a 192.168.AAA.BBB type private IP address to connected local devices. The same AAA value means that the two devices are in the same local network. Different AAA values mean that the two devices are connected to two different Internet routers and cannot connect to each other.

Different devices usually use different port number. For example, a SmartTV uses port 80, while an emulator uses port 8008. An incorrect port number in the URL request will result in the 404 error code. Any random application ID can be used for a test, but a 12-digit Samsung-issued application ID must be used for a production app.

Connect to a TV

A mobile device uses a request URL with the Connect keyword to connect to a SmartTV. The platform supports security-enhanced HTTPS in addition to HTTP. The HTTPS method requires a security BKS file (key store) and an SSLSocket request. This book will only cover a normal HTTP-based connection.

```
private void connect()
{
    // URL Configuration
    String URLStr = "http://" + IP Address + ":" + Port Number + "/ws/app/" +
Application ID + "/connect";
    URL URL = null;
    try {
        URL = new URL(URLStr);
    } catch (MalformedURLException e) {
        e.printStackTrace();
    }

    // Create a HttpClient object and configure protocol
    HttpClient httpClient = new DefaultHttpClient();
    ProtocolVersion protocol = new ProtocolVersion("HTTP", 1, 1);
    httpClient.getParams().setParameter(CoreProtocolPNames.PROTOCOL_VERSION,
protocol);

    // Create a Connect request header
    AbstractHttpMessage message = new HttpPost(URLStr);
    message.setParams(new BasicHttpParams().setParameter(URLStr, URL));
    message.addHeader("User-Agent", "Android-Phone");
```

```
message.addHeader("SLDeviceID", "12345");
message.addHeader("VendorID", "VendorTV");
message.addHeader("ProductID", "SMARTdev");
message.addHeader("DeviceName", "SamsungGalaxyS3");

try {
   // Send the Connect request to the TV (returns HttpResponse object)
   HttpResponse response = httpClient.execute((HttpUriRequest) message);

   // Returns the response code
   int statusCode = response.getStatusLine().getStatusCode();
} catch (ClientProtocolException e) {
   e.printStackTrace();
} catch (IOException e) {
   e.printStackTrace();
}
}
```

Send Message

With the Connect request successfully processed, let's move to sending a message. A similar step to the preceding Connect request will be used, except that a JSON-formatted message will be sent along. Receive a pair of strings formatted type and msg and create a JSON object, convert it to a string, in byte format, and include it in an HttpEntityEnclosingRequest object to be sent.

```
private void sendMessage(String type, String msg)
{
   // URL Configuration
   String URLStr = "http://" + IP Address + ":" + Port Number + "/ws/app/" +
Application ID + "/queue";
   URL URL = null;
   try {
      URL = new URL(URLStr);
```

```
   } catch (MalformedURLException e) {
     e.printStackTrace();
   }

   // Create a JSON object and store type and message values
   JSONObject jsonObj = new JSONObject();
   try {
     jsonObj.put(JSON_TYPE, type);
     jsonObj.put(JSON_VALUE, msg);
   } catch (JSONException e1) {
     e1.printStackTrace();
   }

   // Convert the JSON object to a String
   String body = jsonObj.toString();

   // Create an HttpClient object and configure protocol
   HttpClient httpClient = new DefaultHttpClient();
   ProtocolVersion protocol = new ProtocolVersion("HTTP", 1, 1);
   httpClient.getParams().setParameter(CoreProtocolPNames.PROTOCOL_VERSION,
protocol);

   // Create a Send Message request header
   AbstractHttpMessage message = new HttpPost(URLStr);
   message.setParams(new BasicHttpParams().setParameter(URLStr, URL));
   message.addHeader("User-Agent", "Android-Phone");
   message.addHeader("SLDeviceID", "12345");

   // // Translate type and message data in the JSON object into bytes
   AbstractHttpEntity entity = new ByteArrayEntity(body.getBytes());

   // Configure Content-Type header
   entity.setContentType("application/json");

   // Store the entity object with byte format type
   // and message data into the HttpEntityEnclosingRequest object
   HttpEntityEnclosingRequest entityMessage = (HttpEntityEnclosingRequest)
message;
```

```
        entityMessage.setEntity(entity);

        try {
            Send the message to the TV (returns HttpResponse object)
            HttpResponse response = httpClient.execute((HttpUriRequest) entityMessage)
;

            // Returns the response code
            int statusCode = response.getStatusLine().getStatusCode();
        } catch (ClientProtocolException e) {
            e.printStackTrace();
        } catch (IOException e) {
            e.printStackTrace();
        }

    }
```

Send Image

The Send Image uses the same queue method as the Send Message, and similar steps are used. Store type value and image filename into a JSON object, convert it to a string, and include it in a Multipart Entity object. The image itself is included in the FileBody object. Then package it into an HttpEntityEnclosingRequest and send it in an HttpClient object to the SmartTV.

```
private void sendImage(String FileName)
{
    File path and URL Configuration
    String filePath = Environment.getExternalStorageDirectory().
getAbsolutePath() + "/Download/";
    String URLStr = "http://" + IP Address + ":" + Port Number + "/ws/app/" +
Application ID + "/queue";
    URL URL = null;
    try {
        URL = new URL(URLStr);
    } catch (MalformedURLException e) {
        e.printStackTrace();
    }
```

```java
// Create a JSON object and store type and message values
JSONObject jsonObj = new JSONObject();
try{
    jsonObj.put("type", "upload_image");
    jsonObj.put("msg", FileName);
} catch(Exception e) {
    e.printStackTrace();
}

// Convert the JSON object to a String
String body = jsonObj.toString();
int bodyLength = jsonObj.toString().length();

// Create an HttpClient object and configure protocol
HttpClient httpClient = new DefaultHttpClient();
ProtocolVersion protocol = new ProtocolVersion("HTTP", 1, 1);
httpClient.getParams().setParameter(CoreProtocolPNames.PROTOCOL_VERSION,
protocol);

// Create a request header
AbstractHttpMessage message = new HttpPost(URLStr);
message.setParams(new BasicHttpParams().setParameter(URLStr, URL));
message.addHeader("User-Agent", "Android-Phone");
message.addHeader("SLDeviceID", "12345");

// Create a MultipartEntity object and set up FileBody, StringBody
properties
MultipartEntity multiEntity = new MultipartEntity();
try {
    // Use the image file's path to create a File object
    File file = new File(filePath + FileName);
    multiEntity.addPart("upload_image", new FileBody(file, FileName,
"photo", null));
    multiEntity.addPart("upload_image", new StringBody(body));
} catch(Exception e) {
    e.printStackTrace();
}
```

```
    // Store the MultipartEntity object with Send Image information
    // to an HttpEntityEnclosingRequest object
    HttpEntityEnclosingRequest entityMessage = (HttpEntityEnclosingRequest)
message;
    entityMessage.setEntity(multiEntity);

    try {
        // Send the message to the TV (returns HttpResponse object)
        HttpResponse response = httpClient.execute((HttpUriRequest)
entityMessage);
        org.apache.http.Header[] header = response.getAllHeaders();

        // Returns the response code
        int statusCode = response.getStatusLine().getStatusCode();
    } catch (ClientProtocolException e) {
        e.printStackTrace();
    } catch (IOException e) {
        e.printStackTrace();
    }
}
```

Retrieve Message

The message retrieval process doesn't directly receive a message. Instead, it makes a request for a response object that contains a message, and retrieves a message from the object. First, the process creates an HttpClient object and requests for a message to the SmartTV. Then the SmartTV takes a message from its message queue, and sends it with the response object. Then the mobile device converts it to a string and finally parses it to a JSON-format type and msg pair.

The returned value can be used by activities that need the message, using the Android application's internal broadcast intent method. This entire process is implemented in the following sample code.

The Send Image uses the same queue method as the Send Message, and similar steps are used. Store type value and image filename in a JSON object, convert it to a string, and include it in a Multipart Entity object. The image itself is included in the FileBody object. Then package it in an HttpEntityEnclosingRequest and send it in an HttpClient object to the SmartTV.

```java
// Retrieves a message from the TV
private void receiveMessage()
{
    HttpResponse response = null;
    String type = "";
    String msg = "";

    // URL Configuration
    String URLStr = "http://" + ipAddress + ":" + portNumber + "/ws/app/" + appId
        + "/queue/device/" + "12345";
    URL URL = null;
    try {
        URL = new URL(URLStr);
    } catch (MalformedURLException e) {
        e.printStackTrace();
    }

  // Create an HttpClient object and configure protocol
    HttpClient httpClient = new DefaultHttpClient();
    ProtocolVersion protocol = new ProtocolVersion("HTTP", 1, 1);
    httpClient.getParams().setParameter(CoreProtocolPNames.PROTOCOL_VERSION,
protocol);

    Create a Retrieve Message request header
    AbstractHttpMessage message = new HttpGet(URLStr);   // GET Type
    message.setParams(new BasicHttpParams().setParameter(URLStr, URL));
    message.addHeader("SLDeviceID", "12345");
    try {
        // Request for a message (returns Response object)
        response = httpClient.execute((HttpUriRequest) message);
        int statusCode = response.getStatusLine().getStatusCode();
```

```java
                // If the return code is 200 (Success)
    if(statusCode == 200)
    {
                // Translate the message in the Response object
       HttpEntity entity = response.getEntity();
       if(entity != null) {
                // Convert an InputStream format message in a String value
          InputStream is = entity.getContent();
          StringBuffer out = new StringBuffer();
          byte[] b = new byte[4096];
          for(int n; (n=is.read(b)) != -1;)
          {
             out.append(new String(b, 0, n));
          }
          String responseBody = out.toString();

                // Store the String format message's type and msg value in a JSON object
          JSONObject jsonObj;
          try {
             jsonObj = new JSONObject(responseBody);
             if(jsonObj != null) {
                type = jsonObj.getString("type");
                msg = jsonObj.getString("msg");
             }
          }catch (JSONException e) {
             e.printStackTrace();
          }
       }

                // If there is a converted type and msg pair, send
                // it using the internal broadcast mechanism.
       if(!type.equals("") && !msg.equals("")) {
          Intent intent = new Intent();
                // RECEIVE constant value is used for message filtering by the receiver
          intent.setAction(RECEIVE);
          intent.putExtra("type", type);
          intent.putExtra("msg", msg);
          sendBroadcast(intent);
       }
```

```
        }
    } catch (ClientProtocolException e) {
        e.printStackTrace();
    } catch (IOException e) {
        e.printStackTrace();
    }
}


// Broadcast receiver
private BroadcastReceiver mReceiver = new BroadcastReceiver()
{
    @Override
    public void onReceive(Context context, Intent intent)
       {
       // Use received Intent's Action value for message filtering
       String action = intent.getAction();
       if(action.equals(RECEIVE)) {
          String type = intent.getStringExtra("type");
          String msg = intent.getStringExtra("msg");
          Log.e(TAG, "[type] " + type + " [msg] " + msg);
          // Use Log function to check the message value

       }
    }
};
```

Disconnect from a TV

A mobile device uses this function to request a SmartTV to be disconnected. The request returns the 404 response code if the two devices are not connected.

```
private void disconnect()
{
    // URL Configuration
    String URLStr = "http://" + IP Address + ":" + Port Number + "/ws/app/" +
Application ID + "/disconnect";
```

```java
    URL URL = null;
    try {
       URL = new URL(URLStr);
    } catch (MalformedURLException e) {
       e.printStackTrace();
    }


    // Create an HttpClient object and configuration protocol
    HttpClient httpClient = new DefaultHttpClient();
    ProtocolVersion protocol = new ProtocolVersion("HTTP", 1, 1);
    httpClient.getParams().setParameter(CoreProtocolPNames.PROTOCOL_VERSION,
protocol);


    // Create a Disconnect request header
    AbstractHttpMessage message = new HttpPost(URLStr);
    message.setParams(new BasicHttpParams().setParameter(URLStr, URL));
    message.addHeader("SLDeviceID", "12345");


    try {
       // Send the Disconnect request to the TV (returns Response object)
       HttpResponse response = httpClient.execute((HttpUriRequest) message);


       // Returns the response code
       int statusCode = response.getStatusLine().getStatusCode();
    } catch (ClientProtocolException e) {
       e.printStackTrace();
    } catch (IOException e) {
       e.printStackTrace();
    }
}
```

Introducing the AllShare Framework

The AllShare Framework provides an easy way to enjoy and share media contents (VOD, pictures, music, etc.) between Samsung devices. It provides many convenient features, such as playing smart phone–stored content on a TV without copying it into the TV, using a smart phone to play web-stored media content on a SmartTV, mirroring a smart phone's screen with a SmartTV, and sending files.

This may sound similar to the Convergence App API. But it has its own purpose. While the Convergence App API connects a smart phone app with a SmartTV app, the AllShare Framework shares and plays media contents using DLNA and wireless Internet (Wi-Fi Direct).

This chapter will introduce, among other AllShare Framework functions, playing a VOD file stored in a smart phone on a SmartTV screen. This function allows using the AllShare button to play a Samsung Android smart phone VOD on a TV.

AllShare Framework

Figure 11 -5. Using the AllShare to Play a Smart Phone VOD on a SmartTV

The following methods are used to play a VOD using the AllShare Framework.

1. Device search using DeviceFinder

2. Playing the VOD using AV Player

See the recently published AllShare Framework document.

▶ Note: http://developer.samsung.com/allshare-framework

See below for recommended system requirements for testing the following examples.

Samsung SmartTV	2012, 2013 models
Android Smart Phone	A Samsung Galaxy S3 or later model (with the AllShareService installed)
MP4 VOD File	Ready the /sdcard/Movies/test.mp4 file
Network Environment	Place only one Samsung SmartTV and one smart phone in the same wireless router. Additional TV selection coding will be needed to support multiple SmartTV units. This chapter assumes that there is only one TV. (Wi-Fi Direct can be used.)

Table 11-17. System Requirements for the AllShare Framework

Preparation for using the AllShare Framework

The AllShare Framework requires Android SDK 4.1.2 (API 16) or higher. Verify the Android version before installing the AllShare Framework.

01. Installing the AllShare Framework Development Tool on the AllShare SDK Use the following URL address to download the tool, as you did for the ADT.

▶ Note: http://developer.samsung.com/allshare/repository/android/latest/tool

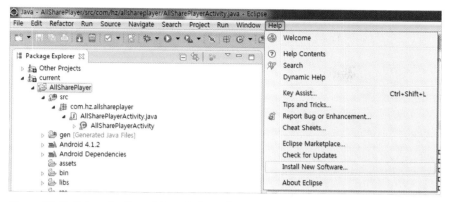

Figure 11-6. Select the "Install New Software" Menu on the Eclipse

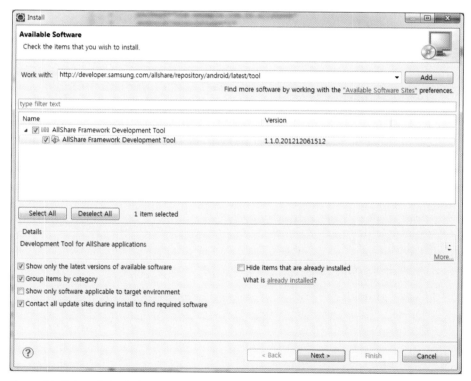

Figure 11-7. Install the AllShare Framework Development Tool

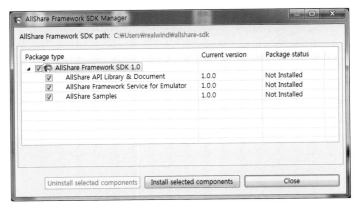

Figure 11-8. Install the AllShare Framework SDK

For more information on installing the framework, visit http://developer.samsung.com/allshare-framework/start and read 1.2. Installing AllShare Framework Development Tool and SDK.

02. Create an Android AllShare Project

After installing the AllShare Framework Development Tool and SDK, the "New Project" menu will have the new "AllShare Android Project" option.

Figure 11-9. Create an AllShare Android Project

For more information on creating an Android AllShare project, visit http://developer.samsung.com/allshare-framework/start and read 2.1, the Creating a New AllShare project.

A newly created AllShare project has the following differences from a standard Android project. A standard Android project can also have the AllShare feature by manually adding access rights and the AllShare library in the manifest option.

Check Manifest Update

```xml
<?xml version="1.0" encoding="utf-8" standalone="no"?>
<manifest xmlns:android="http://schemas.android.com/apk/res/android"
    package="com.hz.allshareplayer"
    android:versionCode="1"
    android:versionName="1.0" >

    <uses-sdk android:minSdkVersion="16" />

    <!-- User permission for using the AllShare Framework -->
    <uses-permission android:name="com.sec.android.permission.PERSONAL_MEDIA"
/>

    <!-- Additional user permission for using the AllShare Framework for
AllShare Cast and Remote control -->
    <uses-permission android:name="com.android.setting.permission.ALLSHARE_
CAST_SERVICE" />
    <uses-permission android:name="android.permission.ACCESS_NETWORK_STATE"/>
    <uses-permission android:name="android.permission.ACCESS_WIFI_STATE"/>

    <application
        android:icon="@drawable/ic_launcher"
        android:label="@string/app_name" >
        <activity
            android:name=".AllSharePlayerActivity"
            android:label="@string/app_name" >
            <intent-filter>
```

```
            <action android:name="android.intent.action.MAIN" />

            <category android:name="android.intent.category.LAUNCHER" />
        </intent-filter>
    </activity>
</application>


</manifest>
```

Check a New Library in the Java Build Path

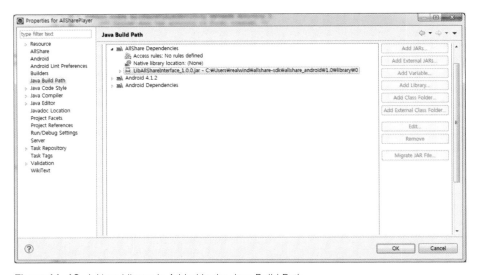

Figure 11-10. A New Library is Added in the Java Build Path

Finding a Device using DeviceFinder

Finding a Device

Use the DeviceFinder class to find an AllShare device. The DeviceFinder class provides the following four functions.

Function	Description
getDevices(Device.DeviceType deviceType)	Shows the list of all devices with the deviceType value.
getDevices(Device.DeviceDomain domain, Device.DeviceType deviceType)	Shows the list of all devices with the domain and deviceType values.
getDevices(Device.DeviceType deviceType, java.lang.String NIC)	Shows the list of all devices with the deviceType and NIC (Network Interface Controller) values.
getDevice(java.lang.String ID, Device.DeviceType deviceType)	Shows the list of all devices with the ID and deviceType values.

Table 11-18. List of DeviceFinder Functions

The following example will use the last function that finds a device with the set Device ID and DeviceType values.

Device Type

The AllShare Framework provides several device types. The device type can be changed after acquiring the device instance. See Table 11-19 for the supported device types.

Type	Device Type	Description
AVPlayer	DEVICE_AVPLAYER	Remotely plays audio/video
ImageViewer	DEVICE_IMAGEVIEWER	Remotely displays an image
Provider	DEVICE_PROVIDER	Remotely provides contents
TVController	DEVICE_TV_CONTROLLER	Remotely controls TV functions
FileReceiver	DEVICE_FILERECEIVER	Remotely receives a file

Table 11-19. List of AllShare Supported Device Types

Let's use the AV Player with DEVICE_ALLPLAYER.

Retrieving Device Information

After retrieving the device list, use DeviceClass to retrieve information for each device. The AllShare Framework provides the following information.

Function	Description	Return Value
getDeviceDomain( )	Retrieves a device's network domain	Device.DeviceDomain List
getDeviceType( )	Retrieves a device's type	Device.DeviceType List
getIcon( )	Retrieves a device's main icon's URL	ex: "http://128.202.198.47:17676/DeviceIcon"
getIconList( )	Retrieves a device's icon list	Icon list
getID( )	Retrieves a device's unique ID String	ex: "uuid:08f0d180-0002-1000-8823-00245491c0ab"
getModelName( )	Retrieves a device's model name	ex: "Samsung SmartTV"
getName( )	Retrieves a device's user assigned name	ex: "[TV]SmartTV"
getNIC( )	Retrieves a device's network interface	

Table 11-20. Information Provided by the AllShare Framework

Once the preceding functions and types are familiarized, review the next example to see how they are used to find a device. The example uses the AllShare Framework to find a VOD playback-capable device.

```
package com.hz.allshareplayer;

import java.util.ArrayList;

import android.app.Activity;
import android.os.Bundle;
import android.widget.TextView;

import com.sec.android.allshare.Device;
import com.sec.android.allshare.Device.DeviceDomain;
import com.sec.android.allshare.Device.DeviceType;
import com.sec.android.allshare.DeviceFinder;
import com.sec.android.allshare.DeviceFinder.IDeviceFinderEventListener;
```

```java
import com.sec.android.allshare.ERROR;
import com.sec.android.allshare.ServiceConnector;
import com.sec.android.allshare.ServiceConnector.IServiceConnectEventListener;
import com.sec.android.allshare.ServiceConnector.ServiceState;
import com.sec.android.allshare.ServiceProvider;

public class AllSharePlayerActivity extends Activity {

    public static final String TAG = "AllSharePlayerActivity";
    private ServiceProvider mServiceProvider = null;
    private TextView mText = null;

    /** Called when the activity is first created. */
    @Override
    public void onCreate(Bundle savedInstanceState) {
        super.onCreate(savedInstanceState);
        setContentView(R.layout.main);

        mText = (TextView) findViewById(R.id.txtLog);
        mText.append("\n\n" + "Creating service provider!"  + "\r\n\n");

            ERROR err = 1ServiceConnector.createServiceProvider(this, new
IServiceConnectEventListener()
        {
            @Override
             public void onCreated(ServiceProvider sprovider, ServiceState
state)
            {
                mServiceProvider = sprovider;
                2showDeviceList();

            }
            @Override
            public void onDeleted(ServiceProvider sprovider)
            {
                mServiceProvider = null;
            }
        });
```

```java
        if (err == ERROR.FRAMEWORK_NOT_INSTALLED)
        {
            // AllShare Framework Service is not installed.
        }
        else if (err == ERROR.INVALID_ARGUMENT)
        {
            // Input argument is invalid. Check and try again
        }
        else
        {
            // Success on calling the function.
        }
    }


    private final DeviceFinder.IDeviceFinderEventListener
mDeviceDiscoveryListener = new IDeviceFinderEventListener()
    {
        @Override
        public void onDeviceRemoved(DeviceType deviceType, Device device,
ERROR err)
        {
            mText.append("AVPlayer: " + device.getName() + " [" + device.
getIPAddress() + "] is removed" + "\r\n");
        }


        @Override
         public void 6onDeviceAdded(DeviceType deviceType, Device device, ERROR
err)
        {
            mText.append("Add - AVPlayer: " + device.getName() + " [" +
device.getIPAddress() + "] is found" + "\r\n");
        }
    };

    private void showDeviceList()
    {
        if (mServiceProvider == null)
```

```
                return;

        3DeviceFinder mDeviceFinder = mServiceProvider.getDeviceFinder();
        4mDeviceFinder.setDeviceFinderEventListener(DeviceType.DEVICE_
AVPLAYER, mDeviceDiscoveryListener);
            5ArrayList<Device> mDeviceList = mDeviceFinder.
getDevices(DeviceDomain.LOCAL_NETWORK, DeviceType.DEVICE_AVPLAYER);

        if (mDeviceList != null)
        {
            for (int i = 0; i < mDeviceList.size(); i++)
            {
                mText.append("AVPlayer: " + mDeviceList.get(i).getName() + "
[" + mDeviceList.get(i).getIPAddress() + "] is found" + "\r\n");
            }
        }
    }


    @Override
    protected void onDestroy()
    {
        if (mServiceProvider != null)
            7ServiceConnector.deleteServiceProvider(mServiceProvider);
        super.onDestroy();
    }
}
```

---

1   ServiceConnector.createServiceProvider – Initialize the service to use the AllShare
    Framework.

2   After step 1 is successfully completed, the onCreated callback function will be called by
    the listener. The function then calls the showDeviceList() function that performs the actual
    device browsing.

3   Initialize DeviceFinder using the getDeviceFinder() function.

4   Register IDeviceFinderEventListener to DeviceFinder. If the AllShare Framework's target device is added or removed, the onDeviceAdded, or onDeviceRemoved callback function is called.

5   Search for AllShare Framework VOD playback-capable local target devices using the getDevices( ) function.

     ✳ **Warning**: The target device search function uses an Ajax request. A slower network may cause step **3** to be executed before step **5**, resulting in devices not found.

6   Target devices not found in step **5** will be eventually found by the IDeviceFinder EventListener's onDeviceAdded callback function.

7   Disconnect the AllShare Framework using ServiceConnector.deleteServiceProvider.

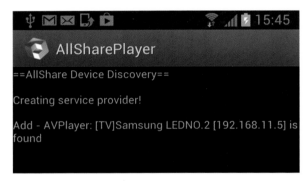

Figure 11-11. A Samsung SmartTV Is Found

VOD Playing using the AV Player

The AllShare Framework uses an item instance to play media files. This item receives FilePath and MIME type as parameters.

AVPlayer Status

The AV Player has one of the following statuses.

Status	Description	Available Actions
STOPPED	Stopped status	stop( ), play( ), seek( )
BUFFERING	Buffering status	stop( ), seek( )
PLAYING	Playing status	stop( ), pause( )
PAUSED	Paused status	stop( ), play( )
UNKNOWN	Unknown status	stop( )
CONTENT_CHANGED	Media content is changed by another device	stop( )

Table 11-21. Types of AV Player Statuses

The UNKNOWN status indicates that there is a network connectivity error and the application or service cannot set the status.

The CONTENT_CHANGED status indicates that another device changed its media contents. An application needs to change the playing UI when receiving this event.

AVPlayer Flowchart

AVPlayer Flowchart

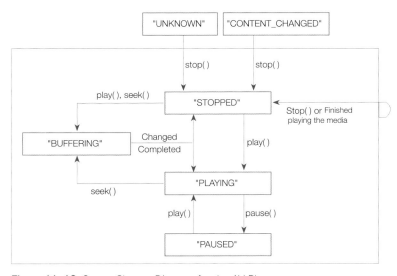

Figure 11-12. Status Change Diagram for the AV Player

```java
package com.hz.allshareplayer;

import java.util.ArrayList;

import android.app.Activity;
import android.os.Bundle;
import android.util.Log;
import android.widget.TextView;

import com.sec.android.allshare.Device;
import com.sec.android.allshare.Device.DeviceDomain;
import com.sec.android.allshare.Device.DeviceType;
import com.sec.android.allshare.DeviceFinder;
import com.sec.android.allshare.DeviceFinder.IDeviceFinderEventListener;
import com.sec.android.allshare.ERROR;
import com.sec.android.allshare.Item;
import com.sec.android.allshare.ServiceConnector;
import com.sec.android.allshare.ServiceConnector.
IServiceConnectEventListener;
import com.sec.android.allshare.ServiceConnector.ServiceState;
import com.sec.android.allshare.ServiceProvider;
import com.sec.android.allshare.media.AVPlayer;
import com.sec.android.allshare.media.AVPlayer.AVPlayerState;
import com.sec.android.allshare.media.ContentInfo;
import com.sec.android.allshare.media.MediaInfo;

public class AllSharePlayerActivity extends Activity {

    public static final String TAG = "AllSharePlayerActivity";
    private ServiceProvider mServiceProvider = null;
    private TextView mText = null;

    private String mDeviceID = null;
    private AVPlayer mPlayer = null;
    private Item mItem = null;
    private String filePath = "/mnt/sdcard/Movies/test.mp4";
    private String mimeType = "video/mp4";
    boolean isPlay = false;
```

```java
/** Called when the activity is first created. */
@Override
public void onCreate(Bundle savedInstanceState) {
    super.onCreate(savedInstanceState);
    setContentView(R.layout.main);

    mText = (TextView) findViewById(R.id.txtLog);
    mText.append("\n\n" + "Creating service provider!"  + "\r\n\n");

    ERROR err = ServiceConnector.createServiceProvider(this,
                new IServiceConnectEventListener()
    {
        @Override
        public void onCreated(ServiceProvider sprovider, ServiceState state)
        {
            mServiceProvider = sprovider;
            showDeviceList();

        }
        @Override
        public void onDeleted(ServiceProvider sprovider)
        {
            mServiceProvider = null;
        }
    });

    if (err == ERROR.FRAMEWORK_NOT_INSTALLED)
    {
        // AllShare Framework Service is not installed.
    }
    else if (err == ERROR.INVALID_ARGUMENT)
    {
        // Input argument is invalid. Check and try again
    }
    else
    {
        // Success on calling the function.
    }
}
```

```java
    private final DeviceFinder.IDeviceFinderEventListener
mDeviceDiscoveryListener = new IDeviceFinderEventListener()
    {
        @Override
        public void onDeviceRemoved(DeviceType deviceType, Device device,
ERROR err)
        {
            mText.append("AVPlayer: " + device.getName() + " [" + device.
getIPAddress() + "] is removed" + "\r\n");
        }

        @Override
        public void onDeviceAdded(DeviceType deviceType, Device device, ERROR
err)
        {
            mText.append("Add - AVPlayer: " + device.getName() + " [" + device.
getIPAddress() + "] is found" + "\r\n");
            if(!isPlay){
                mText.append("  Play : " + device.getName() + " [" + device.
getIPAddress() + "]" + "\r\n");
                startAllShare(device.getID());
            }
        }
    };

    private void showDeviceList()
    {
        if (mServiceProvider == null)
            return;

        DeviceFinder mDeviceFinder = mServiceProvider.getDeviceFinder();
        mDeviceFinder.setDeviceFinderEventListener(DeviceType.DEVICE_
AVPLAYER, mDeviceDiscoveryListener);
        ArrayList<Device> mDeviceList = mDeviceFinder.getDevices(DeviceDomain.
LOCAL_NETWORK, DeviceType.DEVICE_AVPLAYER);

        if (mDeviceList != null)
        {
```

```java
        for (int i = 0; i < mDeviceList.size(); i++)
        {
            mText.append("AVPlayer: " + mDeviceList.get(i).getName() + "
[" + mDeviceList.get(i).getIPAddress() + "] is found" + "\r\n");
            if(!isPlay){
                mText.append("  Play : " + mDeviceList.get(i).getName() +
" [" + mDeviceList.get(i).getIPAddress() + "]" + "\r\n");
                startAllShare(mDeviceList.get(i).getID());
            }
        }
    }
}


    @Override
    protected void onDestroy()
    {
        if (mServiceProvider != null)
            ServiceConnector.deleteServiceProvider(mServiceProvider);
        super.onDestroy();
    }


    private void initItem() {

        DeviceFinder deviceFinder = mServiceProvider.getDeviceFinder();
    AVPlayer avPlayer = (AVPlayer) deviceFinder.getDevice(mDeviceID,
DeviceType.DEVICE_AVPLAYER); // 1

        if (avPlayer == null)
        {
            return;
        }

    Item.LocalContentBuilder lcb = new Item.LocalContentBuilder(filePath,
mimeType); // 4
        lcb.setTitle("");
        mItem = lcb.build();
        mPlayer = avPlayer;
```

```java
        mItem = new Item.LocalContentBuilder(filePath, mimeType).build();

}

private void startAllShare(String deviceId) {
     mDeviceID = deviceID;   // 1
    initItem(); // 2
    registerEventListener(); // 5
    registerResponseHandler();// 6
    play();// 7
    isPlay = true;
}

private void play() {
    ContentInfo.Builder builder = new ContentInfo.Builder();
    ContentInfo info = builder.build();
    mPlayer.play(mItem, info);
}

/**
 * register AVPlayer state changed callback function
 */
private void registerEventListener()
{

    if (mPlayer == null)
        return;

    mPlayer.setEventListener(new AVPlayer.IAVPlayerEventListener()
    {

        @Override
        public void onDeviceChanged(AVPlayerState state, ERROR err)
        {
            Log.d(TAG,"onDeviceChanged  state = " + state);
            if (AVPlayerState.PLAYING.equals(state))
            {
```

```
                    mPlayer.getMediaInfo();
                }
            }
        });
    }


/**
 * register AVPlayer callback function
 */
private void registerResponseHandler()
{

    if (mPlayer == null)
        return;

    mPlayer.setResponseListener(new AVPlayer.IAVPlayerPlaybackResponseListener()
    {
        @Override
        public void onStopResponseReceived(ERROR err){
        }

        @Override
        public void onGetMediaInfoResponseReceived(MediaInfo arg0,
                ERROR arg1) {
        }

        @Override
        public void onGetPlayPositionResponseReceived(long arg0, ERROR arg1)
        {
        }

        @Override
        public void onGetStateResponseReceived(AVPlayerState arg0,
                ERROR arg1) {
        }
```

```
        @Override
        public void onPauseResponseReceived(ERROR arg0) {
        }

        @Override
        public void onPlayResponseReceived(Item arg0, ContentInfo arg1,
                ERROR arg2) {
        }

        @Override
        public void onResumeResponseReceived(ERROR arg0) {
        }

        @Override
        public void onSeekResponseReceived(long arg0, ERROR arg1) {
        }
    });
}

}
```

1 mDeviceID = device.getID(): Copy and store a newly added device's ID from onDeviceAdded. The Device ID is necessary to call an AVPlayer instance that handles VOD-playing using the AllShare Framework.

2 Prepare for the playing and create a List of playback information.

3 Find an AllShare Framework media playing–capable device using mDeviceID, and obtain the device's AVPlayer instance.

4 Create a playback information list using a file path from Item.LocalContentBuilder and MIME TYPE.

5 Register AVPlayer.IAVPlayerEventListener so that it can call the onDeviceChanged callback function and notify it, if the AV Player's status changes.

6 Register AVPlayer.IAVPlayerPlaybackResponseListener to receive SmartTV messages using the callback function.

7 Send the prepared VOD to the SmartTV using the AllShare Framework; play it on the TV screen.

✽ Callback functions listed in steps **5** and **6** are described in the AllShare Framework SDK.

▸ Note: http://developer.samsung.com/allshare-framework/technical-docs/Programming-Guide

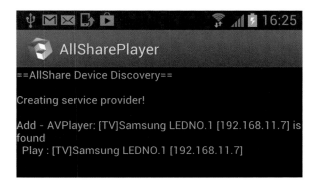

Figure 11-13. A Device Is Found and Selected for Playing

Figure 11-14. A VOD Is Being Played on a SmartTV Using the AllShare Framework

A sample program was created to implement playback of a smart phone VOD on a SmartTV screen using the AllShare Framework. Additional coding will be needed to create commercial software. However, the information was enough to implement advanced media contents sharing and playing capability using the AllShare Framework.

Study more example codes on the SDF and try adding more capabilities.

Summary

The Samsung SmartTV provides data exchange with other devices using the HTTP and UPnP based Convergence. This capability is implemented using the Web API member functions on a SmartTV, and accessed using response headers and HTTP objects on a mobile device. The AllShare Framework is an additional sharing technology that supports easier connection between a Samsung SmartTV and other Samsung devices.

Merging different device types is not the future technology. The Samsung SmartTV already supports it using the Convergence and AllShare.

12

Hands Frame Application 2 – Advanced Version

The Hands Frame basic version was a simple reference application. The upgraded advance version will have additional IME and Convergence capabilities. There are many advanced SmartTV functions other than the IME and Convergence. But these two are the most important functions making a polished application.

This chapter will show adding a login capability that uses the IME to display user input data, and SmartTV – mobile device communication capability using the Convergence.

Login

A standard web service takes ID/password input to access a database to authenticate user login. However, this chapter will simply use the IME to receive an ID input and display it.

Input Tag

An <input> element (for login form) is placed in the Hands Frame's header pane and receives user input data from the IME. An <input> element can receive the focus, as an anchor element does.

Figure 12-1. Hands Frame Application Design

To upgrade the Hands Frame basic version, add an <input> element in the index.html file to load the IME module.

```
<div id="header">
    <div class="login"> ID : <input type="text" id="login_form"
maxlength="5" onkeydown="Main.login.keyDown();" /></div>
</div>
```

While an <input> element receives the focus as an <anchor> element does, it also needs different styles to indicate the focused status. See the following example.

```
#header .login {
    position: absolute;
    top: 20px;
    left: 750px;
    color: #fff;
}

#header .login #login_form {
    height: 25px;
}

#header .login.focus #login_form{
    border: 6px solid #c409d2;
}
```

Next, make the <input> element as Main's member property for easier access, and add a KeyDown handler function to enable it to process remote control key events. The following source code is built on the previous Hands Frame basic version.

```
var Main = {
    category : {
        elem : jQuery('#category'),
        li   : jQuery('#category').find('ul > li'),
        anchor : jQuery('#anchor_category'),
```

```javascript
        },
        content : {
            elem : jQuery('#content'),
            div : jQuery('#content > div'),
            anchor : jQuery('#anchor_content')
        },
        player : {
            anchor : jQuery('#anchor_player')
        },
        info : {
            elem : jQuery('#scene_info'),
            anchor : jQuery('#anchor_info')
        },
        login : {
            elem : jQuery('#header > .login'),
            form : jQuery('#login_form')
        }
};

// Declare an IME object
var oIME = null;

// Shows login status
var login_flag = false;

Main.login.keyDown = function(){
    var keyCode = event.keyCode;

    switch(keyCode)
    {
        case tvKey.KEY_RETURN:
            widgetAPI.sendReturnEvent();
            break;
        case tvKey.KEY_DOWN:
            break;
        case tvKey.KEY_ENTER:
            break;
```

```
            default:
                break;
        }
    };
```

The next source shows implementation of pressing the up directional key on the category pane to focus the <input> element. Observe how the Main.category. keyDown function handles the up directional key event.

```
Main.category.keyDown = function()
{
    var keyCode = event.keyCode;

    switch(keyCode)
    {
        case tvKey.KEY_RETURN:
            widgetAPI.sendReturnEvent();
            break;
        case tvKey.KEY_LEFT:
            break;
        case tvKey.KEY_RIGHT:
            Main.content.anchor.focus();
            Main.category.elem.removeClass('focus');
            Main.content.elem.addClass('focus');
            Main.content.div.eq(index).find('li').eq(content_index).
addClass('focus');
            focused_comp = 'content';
            break;
        case tvKey.KEY_UP:
            if(index == 0){
                if(!login_flag){
                    Main.login.form.focus();
                    Main.category.elem.removeClass('focus');
                    Main.login.elem.addClass('focus');
                }
            }else{
```

```
                    Main.category.li.eq(index).removeClass('focus');
                    Main.category.li.eq(--index).addClass('focus');
                    Main.loadContent();
                }
                break;
            case tvKey.KEY_DOWN:
                if(index < Main.category.li.size() - 1){
                    Main.category.li.eq(index).removeClass('focus');
                    Main.category.li.eq(++index).addClass('focus');

                    Main.loadContent();
                }
                break;
            case tvKey.KEY_INFO :
                Main.info.elem.show();
                Main.info.anchor.focus();
                break;
            default:
                alert("Unhandled key");
                break;
        }
    }
};
```

Category index value 0 means that the focus is already on the top category item. There are no more list items to move the focus up. The program scenario requires moving the focus up to the input element. While not implemented yet, the code will first check the login_flag variable to see if a user is already in to handle an exception, and then will focus the element. Also, the code uses iQuery's addClass() and removeClass() functions to apply the previously defined styles on the element.

Also, see below for giving the focus back to the category anchor if the down directional key is pressed while the <input> element is focused.

```
Main.login.keyDown = function(){
    var keyCode = event.keyCode;
```

```
        switch(keyCode)
        {
            case tvKey.KEY_RETURN:
                widgetAPI.sendReturnEvent();
                break;
            case tvKey.KEY_DOWN:
                Main.category.anchor.focus();
                Main.login.elem.removeClass('focus');
                Main.category.elem.addClass('focus');
                break;
            case tvKey.KEY_ENTER:
                break;
            default:
                break;
        }
    };
```

A case statement is used for the down directional key to move the focus back to the category anchor. Since the <input> element only needs the down directional key and Return key, other keys are not handled. Note that there are no separate case statements for them.

IME Module

Once the focus scenario is implemented using the <input> element, the next step will connect the IME module, as was explained in chapter 10, IME. The following libraries need to be declared in the index.html file to use the IME module.

```
<script type="text/javascript" src="$MANAGER_WIDGET/Common/API/Plugin.js"></
script>
<!-- IME Module -->
    <script type="text/javascript" language='javascript' src="$MANAGER_
WIDGET/Common/IME_XT9/ime.js"></script>
    <script type="text/javascript" language='javascript' src="$MANAGER_
WIDGET/Common/IME_XT9/inputCommon/ime_input.js"></script>
```

The following function calls the IME module.

```
var focusIME = function() {
    oIME = new IMEShell_Common();
    oIME.inputboxID = "login_form";
    oIME.onKeyPressFunc = function(nKeyCode) {
      switch(nKeyCode)
      {
          case tvKey.KEY_RETURN:
                  break;
          case tvKey.KEY_EXIT:
              break;
          case tvKey.KEY_ENTER:
              return false;
              break;
      }
    };

    Main.login.form.focus();
    oIME.onShow();
};
```

See the end part of the focusIME functions that call the onShow() function of the IME object to confirm it.

As mentioned earlier, the Enter key calls the IME module in the following remote key event handling function.

```
Main.login.keyDown = function(){
    var keyCode = event.keyCode;

    switch(keyCode)
    {
        case tvKey.KEY_RETURN:
            event.preventDefault();
            widgetAPI.sendReturnEvent();
            break;
```

```
        case tvKey.KEY_DOWN:
            Main.category.anchor.focus();
            Main.login.elem.removeClass('focus');
            Main.category.elem.addClass('focus');
            break;
        case tvKey.KEY_ENTER:
            focusIME();
            break;
        default:
            break;
    }
};
```

Pressing the Enter key within the input element calls the IME module, and displays the next screen. Note that an XT9 keyboard can be called instead of the QWERTY keyboard shown in the figure.

Figure 12-2. Hands Frame IME

The following function displays data received by the IME module on the <input> element. It clears the element, displays the new input data, and finally moves the focus back to the category anchor to prevent losing the focus. See the following implementation.

```
var form_submit = function(){
    Main.login.elem.empty();
    Main.login.elem.text('Welcome ! '+Main.login.form.val() + '.');
    login_flag = true; // Boolean value that shows if a user is already
logged in
    Main.category.anchor.focus();
    Main.login.elem.removeClass('focus');
    Main.category.elem.addClass('focus');
};
```

The function needs to be inserted in the previous focusIME() function's Enter key case statement.

```
case tvKey.KEY_ENTER:
    form_submit();
    return false;
    break;
```

Note that the preceding simple demonstration may lack some necessary functions. Make sure to see the complete Hands Frame application source code in the addendum.

Virtual Remote Controller Using the Convergence

The second advanced feature is the trendy mobile Convergence capability. While a service application needs more complex and difficult connectivity, this chapter will demonstrate a simple function that controls text messages on the TV application using a mobile device.

The text message to be displayed in the Hands Frame application is "Connecting to a mobile device…" as shown below.

Figure 12-3. Hands Frame Convergence Connectivity

SmartTV Convergence

Use the following element in index.html to display the status message.

```
<div id="convergence_help">Connecting to a mobile device…</div>
```

While the screen shows a connecting message, the message was actually just a show event request by a mobile device. Its initial status is hidden by the next style.

```
#convergence_help{
    position: absolute;
    top: 23px;
    left: 510px;
```

```
    color: #eee;
    display: none;
}
```

The webapis.js file needs to be included in the index.html file to use the Convergence feature.

```
<script type="text/javascript" language="javascript" src="$MANAGER_WIDGET/
Common/webapi/1.0/webapis.js"></script>
```

API and callback functions used in the example are already covered in chapter 11, The Convergence and AllShare Framework. Let's move to the actual implementation. Implement the Convergence in the Main.js file that controls the screen layers.

```
var Convergence = {
    api: window.webapis.customdevice || {},
    aDevice: [],
    init: function() {
        this.api.registerManagerCallback(Convergence.registerManager);
        this.api.getCustomDevices(Convergence.getCustomDevices);
    },
    registerManager: function(oManagerEvent) {
        var _this = Convergence;
        switch(oManagerEvent.eventType) {
            case _this.api.MGR_EVENT_DEV_CONNECT:
                _this.api.getCustomDevices(Convergence.getCustomDevices);
                break;
            case _this.api.MGR_EVENT_DEV_DISCONNECT:
                _this.api.getCustomDevices(Convergence.getCustomDevices);
                break;
            default:
                break;
        }
    },
```

```
getCustomDevices: function(aDevice) {
    var _this = Convergence;
    _this.aDevice = aDevice;

    for(var i = 0; i < aDevice.length; i++) {
        var sID = aDevice[i].getUniqueID();
        aDevice[i].registerDeviceCallback(function(oDeviceInfo) {
            _this.registerDevice(sID, oDeviceInfo);
        });
    }
},
registerDevice: function(sID, oDeviceInfo) {
    var mobileKeyEvent = jQuery.parseJSON(oDeviceInfo.data.message1);
    handleMobileEvent(mobileKeyEvent.msg);
},
sendMessage: function(oDevice, sMessage) {
    return oDevice.sendMessage(sMessage);
},
broadcastMessage: function(sMessage) {
    return this.aDevice[0] && this.aDevice[0].broadcastMessage(sMessage);
},
uploadFile: function(sName) {
    // sName: image file name
    var sUrl = 'http://127.0.0.1/ws/app/' + curWidget.id  + '/file/' +
sName;
    return '<img src="' + sUrl + '"/>';
}
};
Convergence.init();
```

The preceding registerDevice callback function will be called when a mobile device requests the event. This function's oDeviceInfor object parameter contains the mobile's event information, which includes message objects for Show and Hide.

The internally called handleMobileEvent function reads the message and shows or hides the UI component, as implemented below.

```
// Process the requested event
var handleMobileEvent = function(event){
    switch(event) {
        case 'msg_show' :
            $('#convergence_help').show();
            break;
        case 'msg_hide' :
            $('#convergence_help').hide();
            break;
    }
};
```

The source code shows that msg_show and msg_hide messages are used to call the Show or Hide event. The two events messages also need to be declared in the mobile device.

Mobile Convergence

The required Android version Hands Frame application needs the following components

- A utility class for the Convergence connectivity
- An activity class
- XML layout

The utility class holds necessary TV connection information, including IP, port, and application ID. It handles connection and disconnection functions. The activity class is the main source file that defines the TV requesting events and application behaviors. The XML layout defines user interface for the events with Show and Hide buttons. See the source code in the addendum.

Figure 12-4. Hands Frame Android Application (Mobile)

Summary

This chapter added two advanced features of the Samsung SmartTV application—the IME module and the Convergence—to upgrade the Hands Frame application basic version. A production app project would have a more complex implementation, but a simplified version was used to explain the concept. The finished Hands Frame advanced version includes an IME-based login function and a Convergence feature that displays and hides a status message using a mobile connection.

13

Advanced Features

The previous chapters already described the basic Samsung SmartTV application features. This chapter will describe more complex additional features such as the camera and SI (Smart Interaction).

Camera

Samsung SmartTV can use both the internal and an external camera. Let's see how the cameras are controlled in an application.

The SDF provides intensive camera-related API guides, including how to set initial position and size of the camera window, that are sufficient for developing an application with the camera feature.

"Fitness VOD" is a good example that uses the camera feature. It offers "Virtual Mirror" that shows a user's action on the screen using the camera feature, so that the user can closely compare a professional coach and herself. The application is available on the Samsung SmartTV App Store.

Figure 13-1. Fitness VOD Application

A user can also control sizes of VOD and the Virtual Mirror (camera) windows with three preset modes.

Figure 13-2. Changing Window Sizes in the Fitness VOD Application

The SDF's DTV Web Device API provides all camera-related API functions. Unlike the IME or AVPlayer, no complex exception handling is needed to add the camera capability. The API simply supports turning on or off a camera. See below for the list of camera controlling functions.

Camera	
CLSID	clsid:SAMSUNG-INFOLINK-SEF
Functions	GetCameraState
	RegisterEventCallback
	StartCamVideo
	StopCamVideo

Table 13-1. List of Camera Controlling Member Functions

Checking Camera Status

A camera's current status can be checked using the GetCameraState() function, which returns one of four statuses listed below.

Function	GetCameraState
Version	Support from Camera-0001
Usage	GetCameraState()
Security Type	RECOG

Return Value	PL_CAMERA_STATE
	• PL_CAMERA_STATE_DISCONNECTED (Camera is not connected)
	• PL_CAMERA_STATE_CONNECTING (Camera is being loaded)
	• PL_CAMERA_STATE_READY (Camera is ready)
	• PL_CAMERA_STATE_PLAYING (Camera is working)

Table 13-2. The GetCameraState() function

▶ Source: http://samsungdforum.com/Guide/ref00008/camera/dtv_camera_getcamerastate.html

The change in the camera status can be monitored using the RegisterEventCallback function, which returns one of the following three events.

- PL_CAMERA_EVENT_DISCONNECTED: Camera is disconnected

- PL_CAMERA_EVENT_CONNECTING: Camera is connecting

- PL_CAMERA_EVENT_CONNECTED: Camera is connected

Function	RegisterEventCallback
Version	Support from Camera-0001
Usage	RegisterEventCallback (Callback Function)
Return Value	void

Example	<pre>function rCallback(event){
	    alert("Camera Event[" + event + "]");
	    switch(event)
	    {
	        case webapis.camera.PL_CAMERA_EVENT_DISCONNECTED:
	            alert("Camera is disconnected");
	            break;
	        case webapis.camera.PL_CAMERA_EVENT_CONNECTING:
	            alert("Camera is connecting");
	            break;
	        case webapis.camera.PL_CAMERA_EVENT_CONNECTED:
	            alert("Camera is connected");
	            break;</pre>

| Example | ```
        default:
            break;
    }
}

//Register a callback function
webapis.camera.RegisterEventCallback(rCallback);
``` |

Table 13-3. The RegisterEventCallback() Function

▶ Source: http://samsungdforum.com/Guide/ref00008/camera/dtv_Camera_RegisterEventCallback.html

Turning on a camera

Use the StartCamVideo() function to start a camera with initial cam video parameters, including distance from the TV screen's top-left edge, the cam video region's width and height, and screen resolution and quality level.

Function	StartCamVideo
Version	Support from Camera-0001
Usage	StartCamVideo(int positionX, int positionY, int displayW, int displayH, PL_CAMERA_RESOLUTION resolution, PL_CAMERA_QUALITY quality)
Return Value	• **True:** (Success) • **False:** (Failure)
Parameters	[positionX] Horizontal distance from the TV screen's top-left corner (integer value) [positionY] Vertical distance from the TV screen's top-left corner (integer value) [displayW] Width of the camera window (integer value) [displayH] Height of the camera window (integer value)
```

Parameters	**[PL_CAMERA_RESOLUTION]:** May choose between VGA and HD using below options • webapis.camera.PL_CAMERA_RESOLUTION_VGA • webapis.camera.PL_CAMERA_RESOLUTION_HD **[PL_CAMERA_QUALITY]:** May choose among Low, Middle, and High using below options • webapis.camera.PL_CAMERA_QUALITY_LOW • webapis.camera.PL_CAMERA_QUALITY_MID • webapis.camera.PL_CAMERA_QUALITY_HIGH

Example	`webapis.camera.StartCamVideo(0, 0, 640, 480, webapis.camera.PL_`
	`CAMERA_RESOLUTION_VGA,`
	`webapis.camera.PL_CAMERA_QUALITY_HIGH);`
	
	Turn the camera on with its screen displayed as a 640px by 480px window located at the top-left corner of the TV screen.

Table 13-4. The StartCamVideo( ) Function

▶ Source: http://samsungdforum.com/Guide/ref00008/camera/dtv_camera_startcamvideo.html

Turning off a camera

Turning off a camera is easier than turning it on since no parameter is necessary. Use the StopCamVideo() function to turn off a camera. The function returns a value that indicates if the camera was successfully turned off.

Function	StopCamVideo
Version	Support from Camera-0001
Usage	StopCamVideo()
Return Value	• 1 (Success) • 0 (Failure)
Example	`webapis.camera.StopCamVideo();`

Table 13-5. The StopCamVideo( ) Function

▶ Source: http://samsungdforum.com/Guide/ref00008/camera/dtv_camera_stopcamvideo.html

The next example demonstrates turning on a camera and then turning it off.

```
if(it == 0)
{
    webapis.camera.StartCamVideo(21,0,968,680, webapis.camera.PL_CAMERA_
RESOLUTION_VGA, webapis.camera.PL_CAMERA_QUALITY_HIGH);
}
else if(it == 1)
{
    webapis.camera.StopCamVideo();
}
```

► Source: http://samsungdforum.com/Guide/tut00037/index.html

Smart Interaction

What is SI (Smart Interaction)?

While a SmartTV's standard input device is a remote controller, the Samsung SmartTV supports additional TV controlling options with voice and (movement) gesture sensing. Samsung calls this technology Smart Interaction.

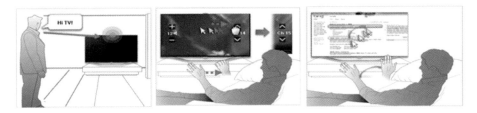

Figure 13-3. The SI Concept

Preparation for using the SI

The Web Device API library is needed to use the SI. Add the below statement in index.html to enable the application to use the library.

index.html

```
<script type="text/javascript" src="$MANAGER_WIDGET/Common/webAPI/1.0/
webapis.js">
</script>
```

Checking the SI Capability

Not all Samsung SmartTVs support the SI. Only the 7000 series or higher models that were marketed after 2012 have the SI feature. Therefore, it is vital to check if a SmartTV has the capability before using voice or gesture recognition.

The Web API's Is RecognitionSupported() member function returns if the current SmartTV supports the SI feature.

Function	IsRecognitionSupported
Version	Support from RECOGNITION-0001
Security Type	RECOG
Usage	IsRecognitionSupported()
Return Value	• 1 (Success) • 0 (Failure)

Example	`if(webapis.recognition.IsRecognitionSupported())`
	`{`
	`    webapis.recognition.SubscribeExEvent(webapis.recognition.PL_`
	`RECOGNITION_TYPE_VOICE, 'smartTV', rCallback);`
	`}`

Table 13-6. The IsRecognitionSupported( ) Function

The SI Voice Recognition

The voice recognition feature starts when a user speaks a preset start command, or presses the voice recognition button on a smart controller. The start command can be changed on the Samsung SmartTV's configuration menu.

Figure 13-4. Samsung SmartTV Controllers with a Voice Recognition Button (Left: 2012 Model, Right: 2013 Model)

The following chart demonstrates how the SI API handles a user's voice recognition command.

Figure 13-5. Voice Recognition Flow Chart: When Initiated by a User's Preset Start Command

Figure 13-6. Voice Recognition Flow Chart: When Initiated by a Voice Recognition Button

Activating Voice Recognition

Once the above preparation is done, set the voice element to "y" in the config. xml file to enable the application of the voice recognition feature.

config.xml

```
<voice itemtype="string">y</voice>
```

Register Event

Use the Web API SubscribeExEvent() function to register voice recognition.

Function	SubscribeExEvent
Version	Support from RECOGNITION-0001
Security Type	RECOG
Usage	SubscribeExEvent(PL_RECOGNITION_TYPE type, String name, function callback)
Return Value	Void
Display on the Emulator	"The voice recognition result is returned with the callback function." (Result of voice recognition is returned by callback function)

Parameters	**type**
	
	- [PL_RECOGNITION_TYPE] Recognition Type.
	
	• Voice recognition: PL_RECOGNITION_TYPE_VOICE
	
	• Gesture Recognition: PL_RECOGNITION_TYPE_GESTURE
	
	name
	
	- [string] Event name
	
	callback
	
	- [function] Callback function for the recognition event Function
	
	<pre>resultInfo = {
	recognitiontype : PL_RECOGNITION_TYPE,
	eventtype :
	"EVENT_VOICE_BEGIN_MONITOR" // Preset Start Command was
	spoken (example: "Hi TV")
	"EVENT_VOICE_BTSOUND_START" // Remote controller's voice
	recognition button was pressed
	"EVENT_VOICE_RECOG_RESULT" // Voice recognition result was
	returned
	result : The voice recognition result is returned as a
	string.
	}</pre>

Example	<pre>function rCallback(resultInfo){
	  switch(resultInfo.eventtype){
	      case 'EVENT_VOICE_BEGIN_MONITOR' :
	      case 'EVENT_VOICE_BTSOUND_START' :
	        var customizeHelpbarInfo =
	'{"helpbarType":"HELPBAR_TYPE_VOICE_CUSTOMIZE","helpbarItem
	sList":[{"itemText":"Channel", "commandList":[{"command":"C
	hannel"}]},{"itemText":"Stop", "commandList":[{"command":"S
	top"}]}],"candidateList":[{"candidate":"Search"},{"candidat
	e":"SearchAll"}]}';
	 webapis.recognition.SetVoiceHelpbarInfo(customizeHelpbarIn
	fo);
	      case 'EVENT_VOICE_RECOG_RESULT':
	        var recog_result = resultInfo.result;
	      }
	  }
	if(webapis.recognition.IsRecognitionSupported()){
	webapis.recognition.SubscribeExEvent(webapis.recognition.
	PL_RECOGNITION_TYPE_VOICE, 'testApp', rCallback);
	}</pre>

Table 13-7. The SubscribeExEvent( ) Function

Event Unregister

Use the UnsubscribeExEvent() function to unregister an event that was previously registered with the SubscribeExEvent() function.

Function	UnsubscribeExEvent
Version	Support from RECOGNITION-0001
Security Type	RECOG
Usage	UnsubscribeExEvent(PL_RECOGNITION_TYPE type, String name)
Return Value	• 1 (Success) • 0 (Failure)
Display on the Emulator	Always 1 is returned
Parameters	type - [PL_RECOGNITION_TYPE] Recognition type to unregister name - [string] Event name to unregister. The event name must be the same name used during the register.
Example	`webapis.recognition.UnsubscribeExEvent(webapis.recognition.PL_RECOGNITION_TYPE_VOICE, 'testApp');`

Table 13-8. The UnsubscribeExEvent( ) Function

An application must use the UnsubscribeExEvent() function and unregister registered events on exit. Set up this exception handling in the window.onunload handler.

index.html

```
<body onload="Main.onLoad();" onunload="Main.onUnload();">
```

main.js

```
Main.onUnload = function(){
    webapis.recognition.UnsubscribeExEvent(webapis.recognition.PL_
RECOGNITION_TYPE_VOICE, 'testApp');
};
```

Event Handling

Samsung SmartTV runs the registered callback function when voice recognition is started. The function receives the event object as its parameter, which returns event type, result, and a few other properties.

The next table lists the event types.

Event type	Description
EVENT_VOICE_BEGIN_MONITOR	User spoke the start command
EVENT_VOICE_BTSOUND_START	User pressed the voice recognition button on a smart controller
EVENT_VOICE_RECOG_RESULT	The TV returns the voice recognition result

Table 13-9. Voice Recognition Event Types

The result value holds the recognized user voice input.

Configuring the Voice HelpBar

The voice helpbar shows available voice commands or status information on the bottom of the Samsung SmartTV screen.

Figure 13-7. The Voice HelpBar (2012 Model) and View All Voice Commands (2013 Model)

Use the SetVoiceHelpbarInfo() function to control the voice helpbar. The helpbar has two modes—embedded and server guide—and receives string type parameters.

Function	SetVoiceHelpbarInfo
Version	Support from RECOGNITION-0001
Security Type	RECOG
Usage	SetVoiceHelpbarInfo(helpbarInfo)

Parameters	**helpbarInfo**
	- [string] Information of the helpbar to be registered
	
	``
	Case 1: Embedded Mode
	helpbarInfo = '{
	    "helpbarType":"HELPBAR_TYPE_VOICE_CUSTOMIZE",
	    "helpbarItemsList":[{
	        "itemText":"Channel Up/Down",
	        "commandList":[
	            {"command":"Channel Up"},
	            {"command":"Channel Down"}]
	        },{
	        "itemText":"Stop",
	        "commandList":[
	            {"command":"Stop"}]
	        }
	    ],
	    "candidateList":[
	        {"candidate":"Search"},
	        {"candidate":"SearchAll"}
	    ]
	}';
	
	Case 2: Server Guide Mode
	helpbarInfo = '{
	    "helpbarType":"HELPBAR_TYPE_VOICE_SERVER_GUIDE",
	    "guideText":"Say the word or phrase you wish to type"}';
	``

Example	```
	var helpbarInfo =
	'{"helpbarType":"HELPBAR_TYPE_VOICE_CUSTOMIZE","helpbarItemsList
	":[{"itemText":"Channel", "commandList":[{"command":"Channel"}]},
	{"itemText":"Stop", "commandList":[{"command":"Stop"}]}],"candida
	teList":[{"candidate":"Search"},{"candidate":"SearchAll"}]}';
	
	webapis.recognition.SetVoiceHelpbarInfo(helpbarInfo);
	``

Table 13-10. The SetVoiceHelpbarInfo() Function

Each helpbar mode uses a different method to process the voice data. The embedded one processes the voice data internally, and tries to match it with one of the registered commands in the helpbar. A maximum of seven commands can be registered.

The server guide mode uses an external voice recognition service. The TV sends the recorded sounds file to the server, and the server returns a recognized result back to the TV. This is a more powerful mode, but it requires an Internet connection.

SI – Gesture Recognition

Before explaining gesture recognition in detail, it will be helpful to start with an example application with the feature. The below is RoyPoy, a Handstudio-developed educational art application.

Figure 13-8. RoyPoy – A Children's Art Learning Application Using the SI – Gesture Recognition Feature

Warning

The Samsung SmartTV's mouse event handling is similar to a common JavaScript mouse event handling. However, it has a major potential problem of losing the focus through a mouse onClick event. This process needs to be even more carefully handled while using multiple input devices.

Configuration

Once the above preparation is done, set the mouse element to "y" in the config. xml file to enable the application of the gesture recognition feature.

```
<mouse itemtype="string">y</mouse>
```

Register Event

Use the Web API SubscribeExEvent() function to register the gesture recognition. See the previous voice recognition event registration for details.

Event Unregister

Use the UnsubscribeExEvent() function to unregister an event that was previously registered with the SubscribeExEvent() function. See the previous voice recognition event registration for details.

Event Handling

Samsung SmartTV runs the registered callback function when voice recognition is started. The function receives the event object as its parameter, which returns event type, result, and a few other properties.

The following table lists the event types.

Event type	Description
EVENT_GESTURE_BEGIN_MONITOR	Primary hand's movement is detected
EVENT_GESTURE_SECONDARY_LOST	Secondary hand's movement is lost
EVENT_GESTURE_SECONDARY_ DETECT	Secondary hand's movement is detected
EVENT_GESTURE_2HAND_ZOOM	User made the zoom gesture
EVENT_GESTURE_2HAND_ROTATE	User made the rotate gesture
EVENT_GESTURE_LIKE	User made the like gesture

Table 13-11. Gesture Recognition Event Types

The result value depends on each event type.

Configuring the Gesture HelpBar

The gesture helpbar shows available gestures or status information on the bottom of the Samsung SmartTV screen.

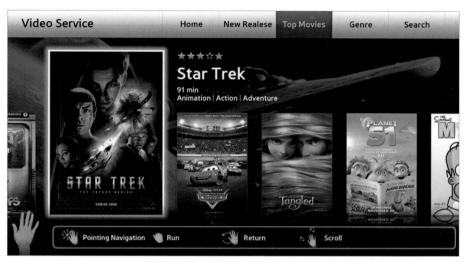

Figure 13-9. The Gesture HelpBar (2012 Model) and Areas selectable by a pointer (2013 Model)

Like the voice recognition, the gesture recognition process depends on the helpbar mode. Use the SetGestureHelpbarInfo() function to control the gesture helpbar.

Function	SetGestureHelpbarInfo
Version	Support from RECOGNITION-0001
Security Type	RECOG
Usage	SetGestureHelpbarInfo(helpbarInfo)
Parameters	helpbarInfo - [string] Information of the helpbar to be registered

Example	```var helpbarInfo = '{ helpbarType : "HELPBAR_TYPE_GESTURE_
	CUSTOMIZE", helpbarItemsList : [{ itemType : "HELPBAR_GESTURE_
	ITEM_RETURN" , itemText : "Go back" },{ itemType : "HELPBAR_
	GESTURE_ITEM_ZOOM_OUT_IN" , itemText : "Zoom in / out" }, {
	itemType : "HELPBAR_GESTURE_ITEM_ROTATION" , itemText : "Rotate
	photo" }]}';
	webapis.recognition.SetGestureHelpbarInfo(helpbarInfo);```

Table 13-12. The SetGestureHelpbarInfo() function

The parameter helpbarInfo object has the following structure. While the below chart treats it as if it is an object data type to help understanding, it is actually a String data type.

Structure	```{ helpbarType: HelpBar Type; helpbarItemList: [{ itemType: Item Type, itemText: "Text" }]; }```
helpbarType	HelpBar Type HELPBAR_TYPE_GESTURE_CUSTOMIZE
ItemsList	Item list for the HelpBar (includes commands list) itemType ItemTypes is the gesture commands to be displayed in the HelpBar. Only events for gestures registered in here are received. HELPBAR_GESTURE_ITEM_RETURN HELPBAR_GESTURE_ITEM_ZOOM_OUT_IN HELPBAR_GESTURE_ITEM_ROTATION HELPBAR_GESTURE_ITEM_POSE_LIKE HELPBAR_GESTURE_ITEM_MOVE itemText ItemText is text to be shown on the HelpBar
Example	```gesturehelpbarInfo = '{ "helpbarType : HELPBAR_TYPE_GESTURE_ DEFAULT"}';```

Table 13-13. Structure of the Gesture Recognition HelpBar

Non-standard mouse events—Slap or Thumbs up—need to be registered in the helpbarItemList to be recognized by the TV. As in the voice recognition, the helpbarItemList has a maximum number of items—four.

File API

The File API is used to permanently store user data (ID, log) to the TV's internal storage (file system) in a SmartTV application. The permanently stored data can be used with File I/O for cache purposes.

All applications share the same directory and can cause collisions by using the same filename as well. To solve this potential problem, assign a subdirectory for the application using its unique IDs.

Let's review the most commonly used functions of the File API using an example.

List of the File API Interfaces

The File API provides the following interfaces.

Interface	Description
Filesystem()	Create a file system instance.
openCommonFile()	Open a file in the application's shared storage.
closeCommonFile()	Closed a file opened by the openCommonFile( ) function.
deleteCommonFile()	Delete a file in the shared storage.
createCommonDir()	Create a folder in the shared storage.
deleteCommonDir()	Delete a folder in the shared storage.
isValidCommonPath()	Check if a file path is valid.
readLine()	Read a line from the open file.
writeLine()	Write a line on the open file.
readAll()	Read the entire open file.

Interface	Description
writeAll()	Overwrite entire contents on the open file.
readDir()	Read file list in a USB storage.
openFile()	Open a file within the application's storage.

Table 13-14. Lists of the File API Interfaces

The File API

Let's review each of the above File APIs in detail.

File System	
Usage	new Filesystem();
Parameters	None
Return Value	A browser file system's instance
Example	var fileSystemObj = new FileSystem();
Purpose	The FileSystem( ) interface creates a file system instance to be used by the app.

openCommonFile	
Usage	fileSystemObj.openCommonFile(filePath, mode);
Parameters	**filePath: String** - File name **mode** - **r:** Open a file. - **w:** Create an empty file to write. An existing file with the same filename is automatically overwritten. - **a:** Append at the end of a file. - **r+:** Open a file to update (both for read and write). The file must already exist. - **w+:** Create an empty file to read and write. An existing file with the same file-name is automatically overwritten. - **a+:** Open a file to read and append. All commands are processed at the end of a file. An existing file can be protected.

Return Value	A browser file system's instance
| Example | ```
var fileSystemObj = new FileSystem();
var fileObj = fileSystemObj.openCommonFile(curWidget.id + '/testFile.
data', 'w');
    fileObj.writeAll(<something to write.>);
    fileSystemObj.closeCommonFile(fileObj);
``` |
| Purpose | The openCommonFile( ) interface opens a file in the application's shared storage |

closeCommonFile	
Usage	fileSystemObj.closeCommonFile(fileObj);
Parameters	fileObj: browser file object - File object returned by the openCommonFile() interface
Return Value	Boolean (to indicate if the function completed the process successfully)
| Example | ```
var fileSystemObj = new FileSystem();
var fileObj = fileSystemObj.openCommonFile(curWidget.id + '/testFile.
data', 'w');
    fileObj.writeAll(<something to write.>);
    fileSystemObj.closeCommonFile(fileObj);
``` |
| Purpose | The closeCommonFile( ) interface closes a file already opened by the openCommonFile( ) interface |

deleteCommonFile	
Usage	fileSystemObj.deleteCommonFile(filePath);
Parameters	filePath: String File path for the file to be deleted
Return Value	Boolean (to indicate if the function completed the process successfully)
| Example | ```
var fileSystemObj = new FileSystem();
var bResult = fileSystemObj.deleteCommonFile(curWidget.id + '/testFile.
data');
``` |
| Purpose | The deleteCommonFile( ) interface deletes a file in the I/O area |
```

createCommonDir	
Usage	fileSystemObj.createCommonDir(directoryPath);
Parameters	directoryPath: String Path for the directory to be created
Return Value	Boolean (to indicate if the function completed the process successfully)

Example	```
	var fileSystemObj = new FileSystem();
	var bResult = fileSystemObj.createCommonDir(curWidget.id);
	``

Purpose	The createCommonDir( ) interface creates a folder in the I/O area

deleteCommonDir	
Usage	fileSystemObj.deleteCommonDir(directoryPath);
Parameters	directoryPath: String Path for the directory to be deleted
Return Value	Boolean (to indicate if the function completed the process successfully)

Example	```
	var fileSystemObj = new FileSystem();
	var bResult = fileSystemObj.deleteCommonDir(curWidget.id);
	``

Purpose	The deleteCommonDir( ) interface deletes a folder in the I/O area

isValidCommonPath	
Usage	fileSystemObj.isValidCommonPath(directoryPath);
Parameters	directoryPath: String Path for the directory to be checked
Return Value	Int ·0: JS function failed (Function failed) ·1: valid ·2: invalid

Example	```
	var fileSystemObj = new FileSystem();
	var bValid = fileSystemObj.isValidCommonPath(curWidget.id);
	if (!bValid) {
	    fileSystemObj.createCommonDir(curWidget.id);
	}
	``

Purpose	The isValidCommonPath( ) interface confirms if a directory exists

readLine	
Usage	fileObj.readLine()
Parameters	None
Return Value	String Returns a new String with the read text value. Returns null if there is no data to return.

Example	```
	var fileSystemObj = new FileSystem();
	var fileObj = fileSystemObj.openCommonFile(curWidget.id + '/testFile.
	data', 'r');
	var strLine = '';
	var arrResult = new Array();
	
	while (strLine = fileObj.readLine()) {
	    arrResult.push(strLine);
	}
	``

Purpose	The readLine( ) interface reads a line from the open file

writeLine	
Usage	fileObj.writeLine(text);
Parameters	text: String - Text to be written on the open file
Return Value	Boolean (to indicate if the function completed the process successfully)

Example	```
	var fileSystemObj = new FileSystem();
	var fileObj = fileSystemObj.openCommonFile(curWidget.id + '/testFile.
	data', 'w');
	fileObj.writeLine(<something to write.>);
	fileSystemObj.closeCommonFile(fileObj);
	``

Purpose	The writeLine( ) interface writes a line on the open file

readAll	
Usage	fileObj.readAll();
Parameters	None
Return Value	String The entire file's contents

| Example | ```
var fileSystemObj = new FileSystem();
var fileObj = fileSystemObj.openCommonFile(curWidget.id + '/
testFile.data', 'r');
var strResult = fileObj.readAll();
alert(strResult);
``` |
| Purpose | The readAll( ) interface reads a whole file |

writeAll	
Usage	fileObj.writeAll(text);
Parameters	text: String - Text to be written on the open file
Return Value	Boolean
| Example | ```
var fileSystemObj = new FileSystem();
var fileObj = fileSystemObj.openCommonFile(curWidget.id +'/testFile.
data', 'w');
fileObj.writeAll(<something to write.>);
fileSystemObj.closeCommonFile(fileObj);
``` |
| Purpose | The writeAll( ) interface writes multiple lines on the open file |

readDir	
Usage	fileSystemObj.readDir(directoryPath)
Parameters	directoryPath: String - Directory path to check. Only for a USB folder
Return Value	- (Array) An array with the file information ·name: filename ·isDir: if the path is a directory instead of a file ·size: file size ·atime: if the file is being opened ·mtime: if the file is being changed ·ctime: if the file information is being changed. Returns false if the directory does not exist.

| Example | ```
var fileSystemObj = new FileSystem();
var usbPath = '$USB_DIR' + usb_mount_path;
var arrFiles = fileSystemObj.readDir(usbPath)
if (arrFiles) {
    for (var i=0; i < arrFiles.length; i++) {
        alert(arrFiles[i].name);
        alert(arrFiles[i].isDir);
    }
}
``` |
| Purpose | The readDir( ) interface reads file listing from a USB folder |

openFile	
Usage	fileSystemObj.openFile(filePath, mode);
Parameters	**filePath: String** File path including the filename **mode: String** r : open a file to read. The file must already exist. Only the r mode is valid.
Return Value	A browser file system's instance is returned. The object's readLine( ) and readAll( ) methods are used to read text from the file.
| Example | ```
var fileSystemObj = new FileSystem();
var fileObj = fileSystemObj.openFile('$WIDGET' + '/testFile.data',
'r'),
var data = fileObj.readAll();
``` |
| Purpose | The openFile( ) interface opens a file in the application |

Table 13-15. Major File API Functions

File API Example

Let's create an example to demonstrate the File API.

Loading the File API

```javascript
// Obtain a file system instance
var fileSystemObj = new FileSystem();
// Data path
var path;

var load = function(){
    // Confirm if the directory exists
    if (fileSystemObj.isValidCommonPath(curWidget.id) != 1)
    {
        // Make one if none exists
        fileSystemObj.createCommonDir(curWidget.id);
    }

    path = curWidget.id + "/data.dat";
};
```

First, create a FileSystem instance and curWidget.id's own directory to use the File API. This example will create the file data.dat in the curWidget.id folder.

Read and Write a File

```javascript
var read = function()
{
    var result, jsFileObj;

    // Open file
    jsFileObj = fileSystemObj.openCommonFile(path, "r");

    if (jsFileObj) {
        // Read data if the file exists
        result = jsFileObj.readAll();

        // Close the file
        fileSystemObj.closeFile(jsFileObj);
    } else {
        result = false;
    }
```

```
    return result;
};


var write = function(val){
    var jsFileObj;

    // Write a new file
    jsFileObj = fileSystemObj.openCommonFile(path, 'w');
    jsFileObj.writeAll(val);

    // Close the file
    fileSystemObj.closeFile(jsFileObj);

    return result;
};
```

Note that different parameters are used for the openCommonFile() interface and depend on the file IO mode. Running the code on an emulator will create the file in an SDK subdirectory, instead of a TV. The existing folder is located below.

▶ **Note:** Samsung TV SDK 4/Emulator/(emulator being used)/commonlib/ (application name)

Delete a File

Once the application is deleted, the curWidget.id folder and files in the folder must also be deleted. Add the next line in the config.xml to accommodate this task.

```
<deleteJS>ResetDB</deleteJS>
```

The ResetDB is a .js file that must be added in the top of an application. The file must include a logic that deletes all files in the curWidget.id that are created by the File API.

```
var ResetDB = function() {
    var fileSystemObj = new FileSystem();
    var directory = curWidget.id;

    return {
        reset: function() {
            if (fileSystemObj.isValidCommonPath(directory) != 1) {
                return true;
            }

            var path = curWidget.id + '/data.dat';
            alert('ResetDB.reset: filepath: ' + path);

            if (fileSystemObj.deleteCommonFile(path)) {
                alert('delete complete: ' + path);
            }
        }
    };
}();
```

HTML5/CSS3

The popular HTML5/CSS3 standard is covered by Samsung SmartTV also. Since Samsung SmartTV application development is based on a web browser, the new standard is well supported.

HTML5

The SDF mentioned that 2012 SmartTV models support HTML5. Its own UI components, Slider and Date Picker, are based on the HTML5 technology. Samsung SmartTV openly supports the following HTML5 elements.

Element	Description
<nav>	A website's navigation block
<footer>	A website's status bar and footer
<audio>	Embedded audio file interface that replaces the previous <object> element
<video>	Embedded video file interface that replaces the previous <object> element
<canvas>	Implement dynamic 2D shapes on a web page

Table 13-16. Supported HTML5 Elements

The Canvas Tag

The canvas element is used to create dynamic 2D shapes and bit images.

```
<canvas id="example" width="200" height="200">
    This text is displayed if your browser does NOT support HTML5 canvas.
</canvas>
```

Control the created canvas element using JavaScript.

```
var example = document.getElementById('example');
var context = example.getContext('2d');
context.fillStyle = "rgb(255,0,0)";
context.fillRect(30, 30, 50, 50);
```

The Audio Tag

The audio element is used to play music or streaming audio files.

```
<audio src="example-sound.mp4">
    Your browser does NOT support the audio element.
</audio>
```

The Video Tag

There was no standard method that can embed a movie on a web page. It required an external plug such as Flash or ActiveX. HTML5 now provides a standard interface to play movies.

```
<video src="movie.mp4" width="320" height="240">
    Your browser does not support the video tag.
</video>
```

The following attributes can be configured in a video element.

Attribute	Value	Description
Autoplay	autoplay	Can set a video to be automatically played
Controls	controls	Provide control buttons such as a play button
Height	pixels	Height of the video player box
Loop	loop	Can set a video to loop continuously
Preload	preload	Can set the video to be preloaded, unless it is set to be automatically played
Src	URL	Video file's URL
Width	pixels	Width of the video player box

Table 13-17. Attributes List of the Video Element

In addition to the above three elements, Samsung SmartTV supports the following HTML5 elements.

Document Type	<!DOCTYPE html>	Supported
Canvas	Canvas Element	Supported
	2D Environment	Supported
	Text	Supported
Video	Video Element	Supported
	H.264 Codec	Supported
	Ogg Theora Codec	Not Supported

Audio	Audio Element	Supported
	MP3 Codec	Supported
	Ogg Vorbis Codec	Not Supported
	AAC Codec	Supported
	WAV Codec	Supported
Geo Location	Geo Location	Not Supported
Storage	Session Storage	Supported
	Local Storage	Supported
Offline Web Application	Application Cache	Supported
	Web SQL Database	Supported
Workers	Web Workers	Supported
Section Element	section Element	Supported
	nav Element	Supported
	article Element	Supported
	aside Element	Supported
	hgroup Element	Supported
	header Element	Supported
	footer Element	Supported
Contents Element Grouping	figure Element	Supported
	figcaption Element	Supported
Text Level Unit Elements	mark Element	Supported
	ruby Element	Supported
	rt Element	Supported
	rp Element	Supported
	time Element	Not Supported
User Interaction	hidden Element	Supported
	Scrolling View	Not Supported
	Contentedtable Element	Not Supported
	Drag and Drop	Not Supported
	Undo manager	Not Supported

Table 13-18. Samsung SmartTV's HTML5 Support

CSS3 Support

Samsung SmartTV also supports CSS3. See below for the details.

► Windows Internet Explorer Test Center: http://samples.msdn.microsoft.com/ietestcenter

3D Transforms

► Note: http://westciv.com/tools/3Dtransforms/index.html

CSS3 2D Transforms	block element transforms	Supported
	inline element transforms	Not Supported
	inline-block element transforms	Supported
	list-item element transforms	Supported
	CSS table element transforms	Supported
	CSS table cell element transforms	Supported
	absolutely positioned block element transforms	Supported
	fixed positioned block element transforms	Supported
	relatively positioned block element transforms	Supported
	property and layout element transforms	Supported
CSS3 3D Transforms	scale	Supported
	rotate X	Supported
	rotate Y	Supported
	translate X	Supported
	translate Y	Supported
	skew X	Supported
	skew Y	Supported
	scale Z	Not Supported
	rotate Z	Supported
	translate Z	Supported
	Perspective	Supported
	Animation	Supported

CSS3 Selectors	:enabled on a fieldset element	Not Supported
	:enabled on an input type=hidden element	Supported
	:nth-child selector with implied step	Supported
	:indeterminate and input type=radio	Not Supported
	:nth-child selector "odd" keyword case sensitivity	Supported
	Chains of :not selectors	Supported
	:not selector parsing no params	Supported
	:not selector with :first-letter selector	Supported
	:not selector with ID simple selector sequence	Supported
	:not selector parsing whitespace	Supported
	:nth-child selector and dynamically inserted elements	Supported
	:not(.class) set and get through OM	Supported
	Parsing check for * ~ :root error handling	Supported
	:nth-child selector with unary prefix on step	Supported
	:nth-child selector and CSS comments	Not Supported
	:nth-child selector and valid whitespace	Supported

Table 13-19. Samsung SmartTV's CSS3 Support

See the below SDF guide for additional information on HTML5 and CSS3.

► Note: http://www.samsungdforum.com/Guide/art00064/index.html

Summary

This chapter covered the camera function that supports virtual mirror, the File API that can store permanent data, and the new standard HTML5. There are many other advanced features that the SmartTV supports. An App Store–published application is much more complex than the simple gallery-style app that was described here. The SDF provides detailed guides for the Samsung SmartTV's advanced application features.

14

Exception Handling

The SmartTV application development needs to handle more exceptions than other platforms. However, understanding characteristics of the remote controlled TV and SDF provides guides that will help handling the exceptions. This chapter will cover a few important points using the Hands Frame advanced version application.

Exception Handling for the Focus

As emphasized many times already, a SmartTV uses a remote controller to move the focus to control an application. The focus must be controlled during the entire time that an application runs. Losing the focus means that a user lost the only control tool to use the application. This can cause erroneous feedback to remote control inputs, or simply no feedback at all.

When the focus is lost while running an application, due to inadequate exception handling, the only solution is ending and restarting the application. See the below example.

```
// Empty an element and output data from the IME input on the element.
var form_submit = function(){
      Main.login.elem.empty();
      Main.login.elem.text('Welcome ! '+Main.login.form.val() + '.');
};
```

The above code was used in the Hands Frame advanced version to implement the login feature. The code uses the IME to get user data for the login form, empty the Main.login.elem element, and enter the received data on there. Although the previous chapter already took care of exception handling for this function, it's shown here to demonstrate a point.

Deleting a subelement of the login element using the jQuery empty() function causes the currently focused anchor to also be deleted. Unless the focus was already moved to another element, the application loses the focus. To solve this problem, set an anchor and move the focus to the anchor.

```
// Empty an element and output data from the IME input on the element.
// Move the focus after displaying the data.
var form_submit = function(){
    Main.login.elem.empty();
    Main.login.elem.text('Welcome ! '+Main.login.form.val() + '.');
    Main.category.anchor.focus();
};
```

The focus can also be lost when the opposite blur() function is used.

```
Main.anchor.blur();
```

The blur() function is often used when calling the AVPlayer or manually ending an IME session. Just remember to move the focus whenever using the blur() function.

```
Main.anchor.blur();
Main.Element.anchor.focus();
```

There are other situations that can lose the focus—loading or ending a module, changing screens, using a pop-up event, etc. The focus will be lost unless proper exception handling is added. The focus is the connection point between a user and an application. Always be careful not to lose it.

Exception Handling for the Return/Exit Key

Unless programmed otherwise, pressing the Return or Exit key ends a running Samsung SmartTV application. However, a common multiple application with multiple screens needs to reprogram the Return key to show the parent screen, instead of ending the application. Since a user habitually presses the Return key to control a SmartTV, a well-designed application will ask the user if she really wants to end the application.

```
event.preventDefault();  // Prevent the Return key event from automatically
ending the application
```

The above function prevents the Return key event's default action of ending the application. See below for how it is used.

```
Main.keyDown = function()
{
    var keyCode = event.keyCode;

    switch(keyCode)
    {
        case tvKey.KEY_RETURN:
            event.preventDefault();
            break;
    }
};
```

Note that the event.preventDefault() function was added in the Return key's event handling. This exception handling is also used to show a confirmation window when the Exit key is pressed. In this case, add the above function and a confirmation pop-up window to the Exit key's event handling code to design a refined application.

Exception Handling for the Player Exit Event

When a VOD playback is complete, the AV Player object's Stop function must be manually called to prevent a system error caused by multiple player modules being called. A second VOD may not play or the application may crash if this step is neglected. Do not forget this exception handling.

```
Main.AVPlayer.Stop();
```

The onstreamcompleted call function should be registered for the AV Player, so that it will be called when a playback is complete. Add the Stop function in it.

```
// Exception handling for the Return key while the Player anchor is focused.
onstreamcompleted: function() {
    Main.AVPlayer.Stop();
}
```

This exception handling is combined with the previous Return key exception handling, as shown below. The AV Player module is declared as a scene and receives key events through its anchor. If the Return key is pressed for the anchor, it should call the Stop() function as well.

```
// Exception handling for the Return key while the Player anchor is focused.
case tvKey.KEY_RETURN:
    event.preventDefault();
    Main.AVPlayer.Stop();
    break;
```

The AV Player may end for various reasons. The above Stop() function must be used for all possible situations. And an application must check if there is any open player object during its exit.

Exception Handling for the IME

IME is an internal Samsung SmartTV module for collecting user data input. Like the AV Player module, the IME module also uses callback functions for various situations. The IME module requires careful handing for the callback functions; in addition to that, it is called with a <form> element. The following exception handlings are necessary.

- Maximum input length
- IME onClose

An <input> element must have a maximum length for the IME module. The SDF allows a maximum of 256 letters. An application may crash after that. Set the maxlength as shown below.

```
<input type="text" id="login_form" maxlength="5" onkeydown="Main.login.
keyDown();"/>
```

The second exception handling is for the IME module's exit. The IME module is opened with the onShow() function and closed with the onClose() function.

If an application suddenly ends without properly ending an open IME module first, the IME module will be forced to close as well. However, this may fail if the system resource was busy closing the application, causing a system error.

To prevent the above situation, the following code must be included in the onUnload function that handles the application exit event.

```
// Event handling function for the application exit
Main.onUnload = function()
{
    if(oIME){
        oIME.onClose();
    }
};
```

Summary

This chapter covered exception handling for the focus, the Return/Exit key, the internal AVPlayer, and the IME. This is not a complete list. But the four exceptions are the most important points in a Samsung SmartTV application. Exception handling becomes easier when a developer familiarizes herself to special characteristics of a SmartTV, such as using the remote controller.

15

From the SDF to the App Store

An application needs to be registered and audited using the Samsung Apps Seller Office and the SDF before it can be commercially published.

First, register the basic application information to be listed on the App Store—app icon, app image, supporting languages—and receive an app ID. Use this app ID on the SDF to register the app package file, after a simple authentication using the name.

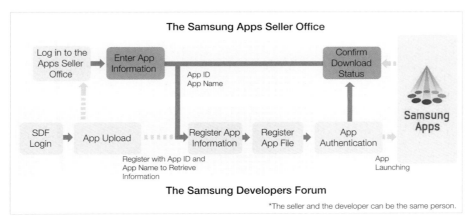

Figure 15-1. The Entire Application Registration Process

The above figure shows the entire application registration process from registering an application on the Samsung Apps Seller Office to receiving an app ID to actually uploading the app package file on the SDF. The two sites are closely linked to support the entire app service.

Registering to the SDF

The SDF manages application registration and point management. The site provides the SDK and API guide documents.

▶ The Samsung Developers Forum Site: http://samsungdforum.com/

01. Click the Register menu in the top-right corner of the SDF.

Figure 15-2. Registration

02. Enter an e-mail address with simple information to create an account.

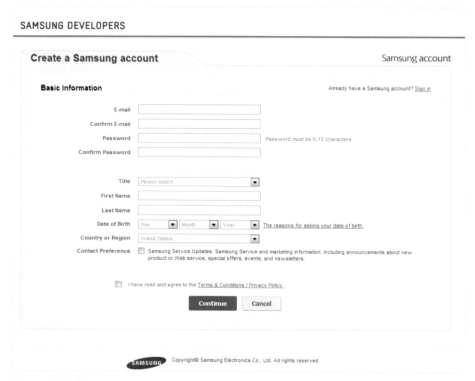

Figure 15-3. Entering Account Information

03. Select the appropriate option from the Student, Professional, or Company account options.

Figure 15-4. Select a Service

04. Receive and confirm an authentication e-mail on the entered e-mail account to finish the registration.

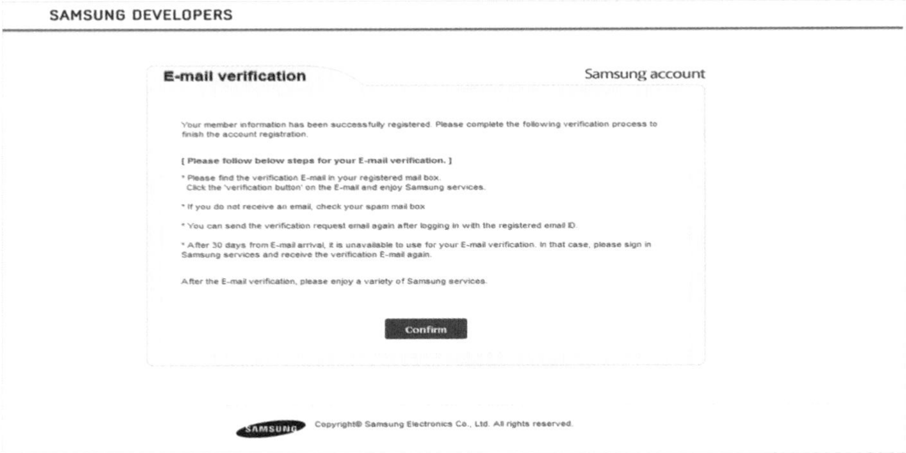

Figure 15-5. Confirm the Registration E-mail

Registering an App on the Samsung Apps Seller Office

The Samsung Apps Seller Office manages application and seller information that is introduced on the App Store, with statistical information and sales amount.

▸ The Samsung Apps Seller Office: http://seller.samsungapps.com

01. Click the "Join Now" button in the top-right corner and proceed with the member registration.

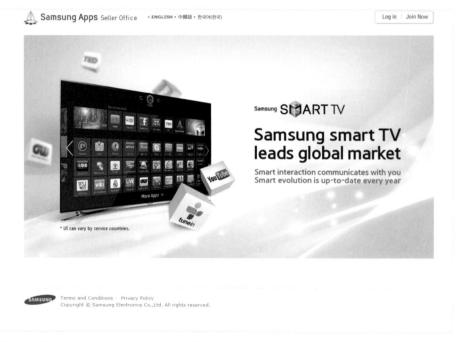

Figure 15-6. The Samsung Apps Seller Office

02. You can also use an existing Samsung account from the SDF or another service. Samsung Group supports the shared ID service that allows one account to be used for different sites.

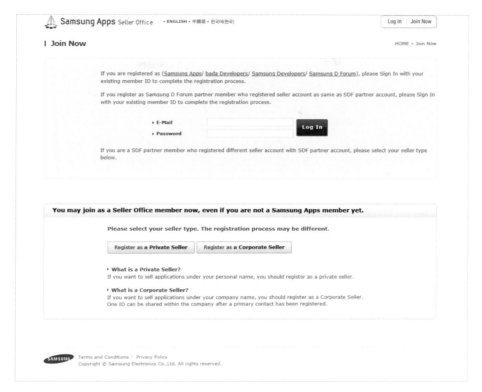

Figure 15-7. Seller User Registration on the Samsung Apps Seller Office

03. During the registration, select between a private seller and a corporate seller option. The corporate seller option requires one main account for all application services, and needs an additional licensing process.

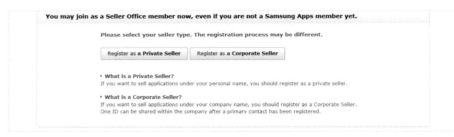

Figure 15-8. Private and Corporate Seller Options

04. Select an application seller type. You can choose both the mobile and TV app seller types.

Figure 15-9. Service Type

05. Enter the basic user information.

Figure 15-10. User Information

06. Read and accept the account terms.

Figure 15-11. Account Terms

07. Check "Agree to All" and click the OK button.

Figure 15-12. Agreement

08. This concludes the Samsung Apps Seller Office registration and preparations to register an application. Let's move on to registering an application.

Figure 15-13. Logged on to the Samsung Apps Seller Office Site

09. Select the "Assistance" menu in the top-right corner of the site. Then select the "Add New Application" submenu to start the app registration.

Figure 15-14. The Main Menu of the Samsung Apps Seller Office Site

10. There are five steps to take to register an application. It also reminds you that the actual app package file needs to be uploaded on the SDF, after the registration.

Figure 15-15. Application Registration Steps

11. Step 1 requires the application name and the support e-mail for the application. Also, the app type needs to be checked. Mandatory fields are marked with an *.

Figure 15-16. Entering App Basic Information

12. Step 2 requires an icon and a screen shot of the app to be uploaded. All the images uploaded in this page will be opened on the Samsung App Store. Make sure to use the correct file specification.

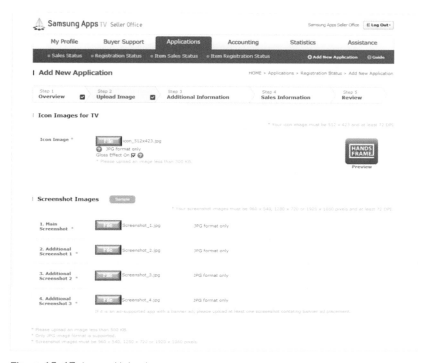

Figure 15-17. Image Upload

The icon and screen shot must be in JPG format. The icon size is 512 x 423. Up to four screen shots of 960 x 540 size can be used to quickly demonstrate the app's purpose and design.

Figure 15-18. Hands Frame App Icon

Figure 15-19. Screen Shot Example 1

Figure 15-20. Screen Shot Example 2

Step 3 requires the application's supporting languages, application introduction, description, and tags.

Step 4 requires market countries and price of the application.

Step 5 reviews all the information entered.

13. There is a detailed guide document that covers Steps 3–5. The guide documents can be downloaded from the "Guide" menu of the Samsung Apps Seller Office site's fixed menu bar.

Figure 15-21. Application Registration Guide Document Menu

14. Once all the registration steps are completed, an App ID will be generated, as shown below. The App ID is needed to upload the actual app package file on the SDF.

Figure 15-22. App ID Assignment

Registering an App Package on the SDF

Now let's move to the SDF and upload the app package and enter app documents.

▶ http://www.samsungdforum.com/

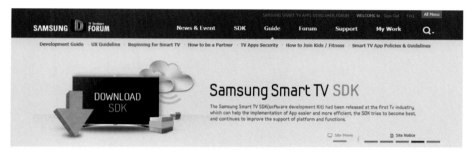

Figure 15-23. The SDF Site

01. Click the "Sign In" menu on the top-right to log in to the SDF.

Figure 15-24. SDF Login

02. Click the "My Work" menu to display the following user information.

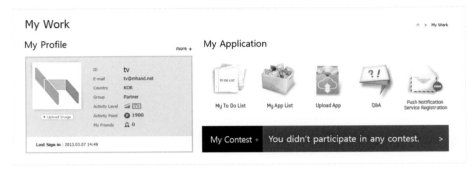

Figure 15-25. The SDF Profile Page

03. Click the "Upload App" submenu of the "My Application" menu. The "Version Up" menu is used to update an already registered application, and the "New Upload" menu is used to upload a new application.

Figure 15-26. The Application Upload Menu

04. A new app package file needs to be accompanied by an application information document. Recheck the SDF guide since the template can be changed.

Figure 15-27. Template for the Documentation

Click the "New Upload" menu to upload the Hands Frame application that was already registered to the Samsung Apps Seller Office site.

05. Click the "New Upload" menu to open the following pop-up window. Enter the App ID and App Name and click the "Search" button to locate the already registered application. The App ID must be the one that was received from the Samsung Apps Seller Office site.

Figure 15-28. Search the Registered App ID

06-1. Step 1 requires basic app information.

Figure 15-29. App Registration Steps

Figure 15-30. Entering App Basic Information

✥ Mandatory fields are marked with an ∗.

The first field is for the app's current version. It is better to use 0.900 versions since the official release requires additional feedback from the Samsung SmartTV App Auditing Team. The seller's site registered category information will be automatically displayed.

Enter "First Release" in the Release Note field if it is the first audit request.

Whenever uploading a new upgrade, clearly describe changed information for the auditor.

"App Description file Attachment" is about the standard template document described earlier. The document needs to contain basic application information, action flow chart, screen design for each page, and remote control key behavior.

See a sample template document in the "My Application" menu for the details.

06-2. Select supported TV models.

	Model Group	Type	Verified Result	Uploaded Version	Opened/Resolved/Closed
☐	11AV-6Group	New			0/0/0
☐	11TV-5Group	New			0/0/0
☐	11TV-6Group	New			0/0/0
☐	11TV-7Group	New			0/0/0
☐	11TV-D6003_US	New			0/0/0
☐	12AV_BD	New			0/0/0
☐	12AV_BD2	New			0/0/0
☐	12AV_PVR_EU_AU	New			0/0/0
☐	12TV_6Group	Change Request	fail	0.906	2/0/28
☐	12TV_7Group	Change Request	Launched	0.906	1/0/29
☐	13AV_BD	New			0/0/0
☐	13AV_PVR	New			0/0/0
☐	13TV_PREMIUM	New			0/0/0
☐	13TV_STANDARD	Change Request	Release approving	0.907	2/0/0

Figure 15-31. Selecting Supported Samsung SmartTV Models

The Samsung SmartTV standard is upgraded every year. And there are many models in each year. It is vital to precisely mark supported model groups while releasing a new application. The audit team will test the app for all marked versions. Carelessly adding unnecessary TV models can delay the audit process.

"Opened/Resolved/Closed" remarks on the right shows the status of programming issues found during the audit process.

- **Opened**: New issues to be resolved
- **Resolved**: Issues already resolved by the developer
- **Closed**: Issues already resolved by the developer and confirmed by the audit team

06-3. Check additional information (codec, supported file formats).

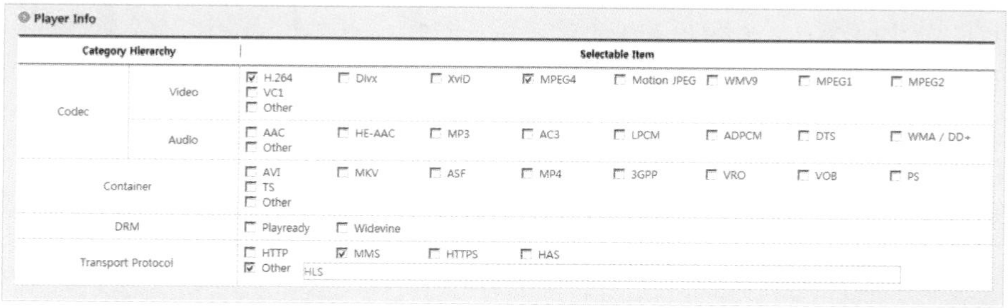

Figure 15-32. Additional Information

06-4. Check the app's purpose and special features.

Figure 15-33. Selecting App Features

Check the app's purpose and special features. Pay attention to major application features such as 3D Contents, Ticker, Gesture, Voice Recognition, and Camera for a smooth auditing process. Note if the application requires an external device as well.

06-5. Check if the app is financially supported by advertisements.

Figure 15-34. In-App Ads

The Samsung SmartTV supports ad-supported apps from SDK 3.5.1, published in June 2012. The Samsung Advertising API must be used to earn advertisements income from the app. Check "Yes" if the app uses the API.

06-6. Check service countries.

South Korea/China	Asia	America	EU	CIS	Africa
Hong Kong	Australia	Anguilla	Aland Islands	Armenia	Angola
Macao	Bahrain	Antigua and Barbuda	Albania	Azerbaijan	Botswana
South Korea	Bangladesh	Argentina	Algeria	Belarus	Cameroon
	Cambodia	Babados	Andorra	Georgia	Congo, the Democratic Rep
	Egvot	Bahamas	Austria	Kazakhstan	Cote d'Ivoire

○ Country ǀ Total : 169

Information of service country is received from Seller Office.
This information should be the same as your app service country.
since the Certification / App Release is based on it. If this information is different with your app service country, please modify it at Seller office before registering(or version up)
the app at SDF.
Your test request might be rejected if the service country information is not in accord with your real service country. Are the above service country information correct?

☐ I Agree

Figure 15-35. Service Countries

A list of Samsung Apps Seller Office registered countries is shown on this page. Carefully mark desired countries. The audit process cannot complete without the correct information.

06-7. Check supported languages.

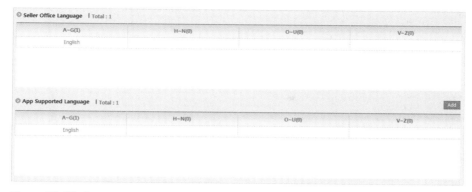

Figure 15-36. Supported Languages

Check if the seller site registered languages information is accurately shown. When all reviews are completed, check the "I Agree" box and move to the next step.

07. Perform a developer self checkup in step 2.

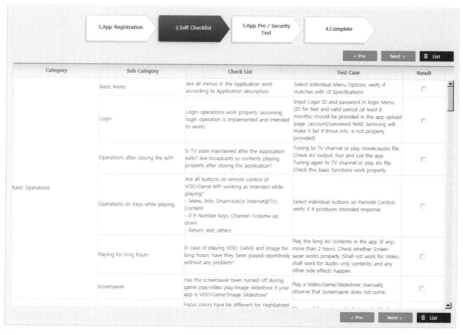

Figure 15-37. Self Check List

The self-checklist is populated based on the previously checked app features.

Perform the final checkup based on the "Test Case" instruction for each of the check list items. A careful review on this step can reduce defects and shorten the feedback process. Once completed, click the "Next" button to move to step 3.

08. Upload the app package file in step 3.

Figure 15-38. App Packaging

The uploaded app package file is first pre-tested for errors, and then repackaged with the site registered information. (e.g., Application ID). Click the "Complete" button when the whole process is completed.

09. The registered app's audit status may be checked on the My Work > My Application menu.

Figure 15-39. My App Status

App Status	Details	Description
Ready	Audit Preparation	
	Ready to Submit	Application is registered
	Submitted	Application is uploaded
In Progress	App Audit in Progress	
	Doc Reviewing	App document is being reviewed
	Testing	App is being tested
Fail	App Audit Failed	
	Reject	App document was rejected for errors
	Test Fail	App failed to properly run
Waiting Launch	Audit completed successfully, and is waiting to be launched	
Launched	Application is launched	

Table 15-1. Descriptions for the My App Status Window

This concludes registering a developed application on the Samsung Apps Seller Office site, and uploading it on the SDF. Please make a careful review of the final steps to avoid a prolonged auditing process.

The SDF sends an e-mail to the registered e-mail address to notify you of errors found while auditing an application. When all issues are resolved through feedback, the application is finally released and marketed in the Samsung App Store.

Application Management

01. The Samsung Apps Seller Office site provides information about all applications registered to the seller account.

Figure 15-40. The Samsung Apps Seller Office Site's Main Menu

02. The "Buyer Support" page provides a customer support interface. Select an application name to see the full customer question and answer it.

Figure 15-41. App Support Q&A List

03. The "Applications" page shows the sellers all applications with sales status.

Figure 15-42. App Sales Report

04. See below for descriptions for the application sales status: For Sale, Suspended, and Terminated.

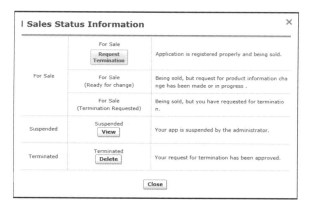

Figure 15-43. Descriptions for the App Sales Window

The Samsung Apps Seller Office also provides "Accountings" and "Statistics" pages for the seller's applications.

Summary

This chapter covered registering a developed application on the Samsung Apps Seller Office site, and uploading it on the SDF. The application auditing may sound strict. But it is necessary for the high-quality application store that benefits consumers, and through increased sales, promotes the application market. Please carefully review the required application registration standards.

Addendum

Hands Frame Source Code

Hands Frame Basic Version
Hands Frame Advanced Version

The Hands Frame application's basic version was developed in chapter 8. The application was upgraded with advanced functions in chapter 12. The application's final version's source code is provided here to give a practical guide for readers.

To the previous Hands Frame advanced version, the latest verson added the VOD URL management technique and a subscene (i.e., Info Scene) management example.

The complete sample application package can be downloaded from the following URL.

▶ Download URL: https://bitbucket.org/handstudio/handsframe/

Hands Frame Basic Version

index.html

```html
<!DOCTYPE html>
<html>
    <head>
        <meta http-equiv="Content-Type" content="text/html; charset=utf-8">
        <title>HG_Layout</title>

        <!-- TODO : Style sheets code -->
        <link rel="stylesheet" href="app/stylesheets/Main.css" type="text/css">

        <!-- TODO: Plugins -->

    </head>

    <body onload="Main.onLoad();" onunload="Main.onUnload();">
        <div id="scene_main" >
            <div id="header"></div>
            <div id="category">
                <ul>
                    <li class="work">Work</li>
```

```
                    <li class="people">People</li>
                    <li class="dream">Dream</li>
                </ul>
            </div>
            <div id="content">
                <div class="work">
                    <img alt="" src="./images/img_title_work.png" class="title"/>
                    <ul>
                        <li>
                            <img alt="" src="./images/1_1.png" class="title"/>
                            <label>What is killer contents? <p>2012.06</p></
label>
                        </li>
                        <li>
                            <img alt="" src="./images/1_2.png" class="title"/>
                            <label>Handmade application <p>2012.05</p></label>
                        </li>
                    </ul>
                </div>
                <div class="people">
                    <img alt="" src="./images/img_title_people.png"
class="title"/>
                    <ul>
                        <li>
                            <img alt="" src="./images/2_1.png" class="title"/>
                            <label>2012 Moments to Remember! <p>2013.01</p></
label>
                        </li>
                        <li>
                            <img alt="" src="./images/2_2.png" class="title"/>
                            <label>People<p>2011.01</p></label>
                        </li>
                    </ul>
                </div>
                <div class="dream">
                    <img alt="" src="./images/img_title_dream.png"
class="title"/>
```

```html
            <ul>
                <li>
                    <img alt="" src="./images/4_1.png" class="title"/>
                    <label>What does your work mean to you? <p>2011.11</p></label>
                </li>
                <li>
                    <img alt="" src="./images/4_2.png" class="title"/>
                    <label>Workplace with true visions, is there one in Korea? <p>2011.07</p></label>
                </li>
            </ul>
        </div>
    </div>
    <!-- anchor as focus for key events -->
    <a href="javascript:void(0);" id="anchor_category" onkeydown="Main.category.keyDown();"></a>
    <a href="javascript:void(0);" id="anchor_content" onkeydown="Main.content.keyDown();"></a>
    <a href="javascript:void(0);" id="anchor_player" onkeydown="Main.player.keyDown();"></a>
    <a href="javascript:void(0);" id="anchor_info" onkeydown="Main.info.keyDown();"></a>
    </div>

    <!-- INFO Scene element Scene -->
    <div id="scene_info" style="display: none;">
        <img src="./images/img_philosophy.png">
    </div>

    <!-- Player container -->
    <div id="player_container"></div>
</body>

<!-- TODO : Common API -->
<script type="text/javascript" language="javascript" src="$MANAGER_WIDGET/Common/API/Widget.js"></script>
```

```
    <script type="text/javascript" language="javascript" src="$MANAGER_WIDGET/
Common/API/TVKeyValue.js"></script>
    <script type='text/javascript' language='javascript' src='$MANAGER_WIDGET/
Common/jquery.js'></script>
    <script type="text/javascript" language="javascript" src="$MANAGER_WIDGET/
Common/webapi/1.0/webapis.js"></script>

    <!-- TODO : Javascript code -->
    <script language="javascript" type="text/javascript" src="app/javascript/
GetPath.js"></script>
    <script language="javascript" type="text/javascript" src="app/javascript/
Main.js"></script>
</html>
```

Main.js

```
var widgetAPI = new Common.API.Widget();
var tvKey = new Common.API.TVKeyValue();

var Main = {
    category : {
        elem : jQuery('#category'),
        li    : jQuery('#category').find('ul > li'),
        anchor : jQuery('#anchor_category')
    },

    content : {
        elem : jQuery('#content'),
        div : jQuery('#content > div'),
        anchor : jQuery('#anchor_content')
    },
    // added Player anchor element
    player : {
        anchor : jQuery('#anchor_player')
    },
    info : {
        elem : jQuery('#scene_info'),
```

```
        anchor : jQuery('#anchor_info')
    }
};



var index = 0;
var content_index = 0;

// stores the currently focused element for INFO Scene
var focused_comp = 'category';



// nested URL array indexed by Category and Contents
var url = [[getAbsPath('resource/1_1.mp4'), getAbsPath('resource/1_2.mp4')],
          [getAbsPath('resource/2_1.mp4'), getAbsPath('resource/2_2.mp4')],
          [getAbsPath('resource/3_1.mp4'), getAbsPath('resource/3_2.mp4')]];



var Player = {
    init : function(){
        try{
            var playerInstance = webapis.avplay;
            playerInstance.getAVPlay(Player.onAVPlayObtained, Player.
onGetAVPlayError);

        }catch(e){
            alert('######getAVplay Exception :[' +e.code + '] ' + e.message);
        }
    },
    onAVPlayObtained : function(avplay){
        // callback function that initializes AVPlayer module
        Main.AVPlayer = avplay;
        Main.AVPlayer.init({containerID : 'player_container', displayRect: {
            top: 0,
            left: 0,
            width: 1280,
            height: 720
        }, autoRatio: true });
```

```javascript
    },
    onGetAVPlayError : function(){
        // error handling function for initializing AVPlayer module
        alert('######onGetAVPlayError: ' + error.message);
    },
    onError : function(){
        alert('######onError: ');
    },
    onSuccess : function(){
        alert('######onSuccess: ');
    },
    play: function() {
        try{
            jQuery('#player_container').addClass('show');
            Main.AVPlayer.open(url[index][content_index]);
            Main.AVPlayer.play(Player.onSuccess, Player.onError);

        }catch(e){
            alert(e.message);
        }
    },
    stop: function() {
        jQuery('#player_container').removeClass('show');
        Main.AVPlayer.stop();
    }
};


Main.onLoad = function()
{
    this.focus();    // assigns the initial focus
    widgetAPI.sendReadyEvent();
    Main.loadContent();    // loads View contents linked to the current Category
    Player.init();
};

// changes contents to match new Category selection
Main.loadContent = function(){
```

```
    Main.content.div.hide();
    Main.content.div.eq(index).show();
};


Main.onUnload = function()
{

};
Main.enableKeys = function()
{

};

// application's initial focus
Main.focus = function(){
    Main.category.anchor.focus();
    Main.category.elem.addClass('focus');
    Main.category.li.eq(index).addClass('focus');
};

Main.category.keyDown = function()
{
    var keyCode = event.keyCode;

    switch(keyCode)
    {
        case tvKey.KEY_RETURN:
            widgetAPI.sendReturnEvent();
            break;
        case tvKey.KEY_RIGHT:
            Main.content.anchor.focus();
            Main.category.elem.removeClass('focus');
            Main.content.elem.addClass('focus');
            Main.content.div.eq(index).find('li').eq(content_index).
addClass('focus');
            focused_comp = 'content';
            break;
```

```
        case tvKey.KEY_UP:
            if(index > 0){
                Main.category.li.eq(index).removeClass('focus');
                Main.category.li.eq(--index).addClass('focus');
                Main.loadContent();
            }
            break;
        case tvKey.KEY_DOWN:
            if(index < Main.category.li.size() - 1){
                Main.category.li.eq(index).removeClass('focus');
                Main.category.li.eq(++index).addClass('focus');
                Main.loadContent();
            }
            break;
        case tvKey.KEY_INFO :
            Main.info.elem.show();
            Main.info.anchor.focus();
            break;
        default:
            alert("Unhandled key");
            break;
    }
};


Main.content.keyDown = function()
{
    var keyCode = event.keyCode;

    switch(keyCode)
    {
        case tvKey.KEY_RETURN:
            widgetAPI.sendReturnEvent();
            break;
        case tvKey.KEY_LEFT:
            if(content_index == 1){
                Main.content.div.eq(index).find('li').eq(content_index).
removeClass('focus');
                Main.content.div.eq(index).find('li').eq(--content_index).
addClass('focus');
```

```
            }else{
                Main.category.anchor.focus();
                Main.content.elem.removeClass('focus');
                Main.category.elem.addClass('focus');
                focused_comp = 'category';
            }
            break;
        case tvKey.KEY_RIGHT:
            if(content_index == 0){
                Main.content.div.eq(index).find('li').eq(content_index).
removeClass('focus');
                Main.content.div.eq(index).find('li').eq(++content_index).
addClass('focus');
            }else{
                return false;
            }
            break;
        case tvKey.KEY_ENTER:
            Player.play();
            Main.player.anchor.focus();
            break;
        case tvKey.KEY_INFO :
            Main.info.elem.show();
            Main.info.anchor.focus();
            break;
        default:
            break;
    }
};


Main.player.keyDown = function()
{
    var keyCode = event.keyCode;
    switch(keyCode)
    {
        case tvKey.KEY_RETURN:
            event.preventDefault();
            Player.stop();
```

```
            Main.content.anchor.focus();
            break;
        case tvKey.KEY_PLAY:
            Player.play();
            break;
        case tvKey.KEY_STOP:
            Player.stop();
            Main.content.anchor.focus();
            break;
        default:
            break;
    }
};


Main.info.keyDown = function()
{
    var keyCode = event.keyCode;

    switch(keyCode)
    {
        case tvKey.KEY_RETURN:
            event.preventDefault();
            Main.info.elem.hide();
            if(focused_comp=='category'){
                Main.category.anchor.focus();
            }else if(focused_comp=='content'){
                Main.content.anchor.focus();
            }
            break;
        default:
            break;
    }
};
```

```
function getAbsPath(linkString) {

    var sPath = null;
    var sLocation = window.location.href;
    var sRoot = sLocation.substring(0, sLocation.lastIndexOf('/') + 1);

    sLocation = unescape(sLocation);
    sRoot = unescape(sRoot);

    if (sRoot.indexOf('file://localhost/') != -1 && (sLocation.indexOf('C:') !=
-1 || sLocation.indexOf('D:') != -1)) {
        sPath = sRoot.split('file://localhost/')[1].replace(/\\/g, '/');
    } else if (sRoot.indexOf('file://localhost/') != -1) {
        sPath = '/' + sRoot.split('file://localhost/')[1];
    } else if (sRoot.indexOf('file://C/') != -1 || sRoot.indexOf('file://c/')
!= -1) {
        sPath = 'C://' + (sRoot.indexOf('file://C/') != -1 ? sRoot.
split('file://C/')[1] : sRoot.split('file://c/')[1]);
    } else if (sRoot.indexOf('file://D/') != -1 || sRoot.indexOf('file://d/')
!= -1) {
        sPath = 'D://' + (sRoot.indexOf('file://D/') != -1 ? sRoot.
split('file://D/')[1] : sRoot.split('file://d/')[1]);
    } else {
        sPath = sRoot;
    }

    return sPath+linkString;
}
```

```
*
{
    padding: 0;
    margin: 0;
```

```css
    border: 0;
}

/* Layout */
body
{
    width: 1280px;
    height: 720px;
    overflow: hidden;
}

#scene_main{
    display: inline-block;
    width: 1280px;
    height: 720px;
    background : url("../../images/bg_main.jpg") no-repeat;
}

#header {
    height: 65px;
}

#header .slogan{
    float: left;
}

#header .appName{
    float: right;
}

#category {
    float: left;
    width: 235px;
    position: absolute;
    top: 87px;
}
```

```css
#category ul{
    list-style: none;
}

#category ul li{
    width: 235px;
    height: 50px;
    color: #fff;
    font-size: 20px;
    line-height: 50px;
    text-align: center;
}

#category.focus ul li.focus{
    color: #fff;
    background: url("../../images/btn_menu.png") top;
}

#category.focus ul li.selected{
    color: #c62ad3;
    background: url("../../images/btn_menu.png") bottom;
}

#content{
    float: right;
    position: absolute;
    left: 313px;
    top: 92px;
    width: 900px;
}

#content  > div{
    width: 100%;
    display: none;
}

#content  > div > div.title{
    display: inline-block;
```

```css
    width: 380px;
    height: 23px;
}


#content.focus  > div{
    color: red;
}


#content ul {
    list-style: none;
    position: relative;
    top: 35px;
}


#content ul li{
    float: left;
    width: 450px;
}


#content ul li img{
    width: 394px;
    height: 219px;
}


#content.focus ul li.focus img{
    border: 6px solid #c409d2;


}


#content ul li label{
    font-size: 24px;

    color: #fff;
    position: relative;
    display: block;
    top: 10px;
}
```

```css
#content ul li label p{
    font-size: 18px;
    color: #acacac;
}

#scene_info{
    width: 1280px;
    height: 650px;
    background: #242424;
    position: absolute;
    top: 70px;
}

#scene_info img{
    position: relative;
    top: 50px;
    left: 15px;
}


#player_container {
    position: absolute;
    width: 1280px;
    height: 720px;
    opacity: 0;
     left: 0;
     top: 0;
}

#player_container.show {
    opacity: 1;
}
```

Hands Frame Advanced Version

```
<!DOCTYPE html>
<html>
    <head>
        <meta http-equiv="Content-Type" content="text/html; charset=utf-8">
        <title>HG_Layout</title>

        <!-- TODO : Style sheets code -->
        <link rel="stylesheet" href="app/stylesheets/Main.css" type="text/
css">

        <!-- TODO: Plugins -->

    </head>

    <body onload="Main.onLoad();" onunload="Main.onUnload();">

        <!-- Main Scene element -->
        <div id="scene_main" style="display: block;">
            <div id="convergence_help">Connecting to a Mobile Device…</div>
            <div id="header">
                <div class="login"> ID :  <input type="text" id="login_form"
maxlength="5" onkeydown="Main.login.keyDown();"/></div>
            </div>
            <div id="category">
                <ul>
                    <li class="work">Work</li>
                    <li class="people">People</li>
                    <li class="dream">Dream</li>
                </ul>
            </div>
                    <div id="content">
                <div class="work">
                    <img alt="" src="./images/img_title_work.png" class="title"/>
                    <ul>
                        <li>
```

```
                                    <img alt="" src="./images/1_1.png" class="title"/>
                                    <label>What is killer contents? <p>2012.06</p></
label>
                        </li>
                        <li>
                            <img alt="" src="./images/1_2.png" class="title"/>
                            <label>Handmade application <p>2012.05</p></label>
                        </li>
                    </ul>
                </div>
                <div class="people">
                    <img alt="" src="./images/img_title_people.png"
class="title"/>
                    <ul>
                        <li>
                            <img alt="" src="./images/2_1.png" class="title"/>
                            <label>2012 Moments to Remember! <p>2013.01</p></
label>
                        </li>
                        <li>
                            <img alt="" src="./images/2_2.png" class="title"/>
                            <label>People<p>2011.01</p></label>
                        </li>
                    </ul>
                </div>
                <div class="dream">
                    <img alt="" src="./images/img_title_dream.png"
class="title"/>
                    <ul>
                        <li>
                            <img alt="" src="./images/4_1.png" class="title"/>
                            <label>What does your work mean to you? <p>2011.11</
p></label>
                        </li>
                        <li>
                            <img alt="" src="./images/4_2.png" class="title"/>
                            <label>Workplace with true visions, is there one in
Korea? <p>2011.07</p></label>
```

```html
            </li>
          </ul>
        </div>
      </div>
      <!-- anchor as focus for key events -->
      <a href="javascript:void(0);" id="anchor_category" onkeydown="Main.
category.keyDown();"></a>
      <a href="javascript:void(0);" id="anchor_content" onkeydown="Main.
content.keyDown();"></a>
      <a href="javascript:void(0);" id="anchor_player" onkeydown="Main.
player.keyDown();"></a>
      <a href="javascript:void(0);" id="anchor_info" onkeydown="Main.
info.keyDown();"></a>
    </div>

    <!-- INFO Scene element -->
    <div id="scene_info" style="display: none;">
      <img src="./images/img_philosophy.png">
    </div>

    <div id="player_container"></div>
  </body>

  <!-- TODO : Common API -->
  <script type="text/javascript" src="$MANAGER_WIDGET/Common/API/TVKeyValue.
js"></script>
  <script type="text/javascript" src="$MANAGER_WIDGET/Common/API/Widget.
js"></script>
  <script type="text/javascript" src="$MANAGER_WIDGET/Common/API/Plugin.
js"></script>
  <script type="text/javascript" src="$MANAGER_WIDGET/Common/Plugin/Define.
js"></script>

  <!-- IME Module -->
  <script type="text/javascript" language='javascript' src="$MANAGER_WIDGET/
Common/IME_XT9/ime.js"></script>
  <script type="text/javascript" language='javascript' src="$MANAGER_WIDGET/
Common/IME_XT9/inputCommon/ime_input.js"></script>
```

```
    <script type='text/javascript' language='javascript' src='$MANAGER_WIDGET/
Common/jquery.js'></script>
    <script type="text/javascript" language="javascript" src="$MANAGER_WIDGET/
Common/webapi/1.0/webapis.js"></script>

    <!-- TODO : Javascript code -->
    <script language="javascript" type="text/javascript" src="app/javascript/
GetPath.js"></script>
    <script language="javascript" type="text/javascript" src="app/javascript/
Main.js"></script>
</html>
```

Main.js

```
var widgetAPI = new Common.API.Widget();
var tvKey = new Common.API.TVKeyValue();

var Main = {
    category : {
        elem : jQuery('#category'),
        li    : jQuery('#category').find('ul > li'),
        anchor : jQuery('#anchor_category'),
    },
    content : {
        elem : jQuery('#content'),
        div : jQuery('#content > div'),
        anchor : jQuery('#anchor_content')
    },
    player : {
        anchor : jQuery('#anchor_player')
    },
    info : {
        elem : jQuery('#scene_info'),
        anchor : jQuery('#anchor_info')
    },
    login : {
```

```
        elem : jQuery('#header > .login'),
        form : jQuery('#login_form')
    }
};

// declares an IME object
var oIME = null;

// toggles login status
var login_flag = false;


var index = 0;
var content_index = 0;
var focused_comp = 'category'; // stores the currently focused element for
INFO Scene


// nested URL array indexed by Category and Contents
var url = [[getAbsPath('resource/1_1.mp4'), getAbsPath('resource/1_2.mp4')],
           [getAbsPath('resource/2_1.mp4'), getAbsPath('resource/2_2.mp4')],
           [getAbsPath('resource/3_1.mp4'), getAbsPath('resource/3_2.mp4')]];

var Player = {
        init : function(){
            try{
                var playerInstance = webapis.avplay;
                playerInstance.getAVPlay(Player.onAVPlayObtained, Player.
onGetAVPlayError);

            }catch(e){
                alert('######getAVplay Exception :[' +e.code + '] ' + e.message);
            }
        },
        onAVPlayObtained : function(avplay){
            // callback function that initializes AVPlayer module
            Main.AVPlayer = avplay;
```

```
        Main.AVPlayer.init({zIndex : 2, containerID : 'player_container',
displayRect: {
                top: 0,
                left: 0,
                width: 1280,
                height: 720
            }, autoRatio: true });
        },

        onGetAVPlayError : function(){
            // error handling function for initializing AVPlayer module
            alert('######onGetAVPlayError: ' + error.message);
        },

        onError : function(){
            alert('######onError: ');
        },

        onSuccess : function(){
            alert('######onSuccess: ');
        },

        play: function() {
            try{
                alert('url[index][content_index] : !!!!!!!!!!!'+url[index]
[content_index]);

                jQuery('#player_container').addClass('show');
                Main.AVPlayer.open(url[index][content_index]);
                Main.AVPlayer.play(Player.onSuccess, Player.onError);

            }catch(e){
                alert(e.message);
            }
        },

        stop: function() {
            jQuery('#player_container').removeClass('show');
            Main.AVPlayer.stop();
        }
};


Main.onLoad = function()
{
```

```
    this.focus();    // assigns the initial focus
    widgetAPI.sendReadyEvent();
    Main.loadContent();    // loads View contents linked to the current Category
    Player.init(); // initializes Player module
};


Main.loadContent = function(){
    jQuery('#content').find('div').hide();
    jQuery('#content').find('div').eq(index).show();
};


// event handling function for the application exit event
Main.onUnload = function()
{
    if(oIME){
        oIME.onClose();
    }
};
Main.enableKeys = function()
{

};


Main.focus = function(){
    Main.category.anchor.focus();
    Main.category.elem.addClass('focus');
    Main.category.li.eq(index).addClass('focus');

};


Main.category.keyDown = function()
{
    var keyCode = event.keyCode;

    switch(keyCode)
    {
        case tvKey.KEY_RETURN:
            widgetAPI.sendReturnEvent();
            break;
```

```
        case tvKey.KEY_LEFT:
            break;
        case tvKey.KEY_RIGHT:
            Main.content.anchor.focus();
            Main.category.elem.removeClass('focus');
            Main.content.elem.addClass('focus');
            Main.content.div.eq(index).find('li').eq(content_index).
addClass('focus');
            focused_comp = 'content';
            break;
        case tvKey.KEY_UP:
            if(index == 0){
                if(!login_flag){
                    Main.login.form.focus();
                    Main.category.elem.removeClass('focus');
                    Main.login.elem.addClass('focus');
                }
            }else{
                Main.category.li.eq(index).removeClass('focus');
                Main.category.li.eq(--index).addClass('focus');
                Main.loadContent();
            }
            break;
        case tvKey.KEY_DOWN:
            if(index < Main.category.li.size() - 1){
                Main.category.li.eq(index).removeClass('focus');
                Main.category.li.eq(++index).addClass('focus');

                Main.loadContent();
            }
            break;
        case tvKey.KEY_INFO :
            Main.info.elem.show();
            Main.info.anchor.focus();
            break;
        default:
            alert("Unhandled key");
```

```
            break;
    }
};


Main.content.keyDown = function()
{
    var keyCode = event.keyCode;

    switch(keyCode)
    {
        case tvKey.KEY_RETURN:
        case tvKey.KEY_PANEL_RETURN:
            widgetAPI.sendReturnEvent();
            break;
        case tvKey.KEY_LEFT:
            if(content_index == 1){
                Main.content.div.eq(index).find('li').eq(content_index).
removeClass('focus');
                Main.content.div.eq(index).find('li').eq(--content_index).
addClass('focus');
            }else{
                Main.category.anchor.focus();
                Main.content.elem.removeClass('focus');
                Main.category.elem.addClass('focus');
                focused_comp = 'category';
            }
            break;
        case tvKey.KEY_RIGHT:
            if(content_index == 0){
                Main.content.div.eq(index).find('li').eq(content_index).
removeClass('focus');
                Main.content.div.eq(index).find('li').eq(++content_index).
addClass('focus');
            }else{
                return false;
            }
            break;
```

```
            case tvKey.KEY_ENTER:
                Player.play();
                Main.player.anchor.focus();
                break;
            case tvKey.KEY_INFO :
                Main.info.elem.show();
                Main.info.anchor.focus();
                break;
            default:
                break;
        }
    };


    Main.player.keyDown = function()
    {
        var keyCode = event.keyCode;

        switch(keyCode)
        {
            case tvKey.KEY_RETURN:
                event.preventDefault();
                Player.stop();
                Main.content.anchor.focus();
                break;
            case tvKey.KEY_PLAY:
                Player.play();
                break;
            case tvKey.KEY_STOP:
                Player.stop();
                Main.content.anchor.focus();
                break;
            default:
                break;
        }
    };


    Main.info.keyDown = function()
    {
```

```
    var keyCode = event.keyCode;

    switch(keyCode)
    {
        case tvKey.KEY_RETURN:
            event.preventDefault();
            Main.info.elem.hide();
            if(focused_comp=='category'){
                Main.category.anchor.focus();
            }else if(focused_comp=='content'){
                Main.content.anchor.focus();
            }
            break;
        default:
            break;
    }
};
Main.login.keyDown = function(){
    var keyCode = event.keyCode;

    switch(keyCode)
    {
        case tvKey.KEY_RETURN:
            event.preventDefault();
            widgetAPI.sendReturnEvent();
        break;
        case tvKey.KEY_DOWN:
            Main.category.anchor.focus();
            Main.login.elem.removeClass('focus');
            Main.category.elem.addClass('focus');
            break;
        case tvKey.KEY_ENTER:
            focusIME();
            break;
        default:
            break;
    }
```

```
};


var focusIME = function() {
    oIME = new IMEShell_Common();
    oIME.inputboxID = "login_form";
    oIME.onKeyPressFunc = function(nKeyCode) {
        switch(nKeyCode)
        {
            case tvKey.KEY_RETURN:
                break;
            case tvKey.KEY_EXIT:
                break;
            case tvKey.KEY_ENTER:
                form_submit();
                return false;
                break;
        }
    };

    Main.login.form.focus();
    oIME.onShow();
};


var form_submit = function(){
    Main.login.elem.empty();
    Main.login.elem.text('Welcome ! '+Main.login.form.val() + '.');

    login_flag = true;     // toggles login status

    Main.category.anchor.focus();
    Main.login.elem.removeClass('focus');
    Main.category.elem.addClass('focus');
};


var Convergence = {
    api: window.webapis.customdevice || {},
    aDevice: [],
```

```
init: function() {
    this.api.registerManagerCallback(Convergence.registerManager);
    this.api.getCustomDevices(Convergence.getCustomDevices);
},
registerManager: function(oManagerEvent) {
    var _this = Convergence;
    switch(oManagerEvent.eventType) {
        case _this.api.MGR_EVENT_DEV_CONNECT:
            _this.api.getCustomDevices(Convergence.getCustomDevices);
            break;
        case _this.api.MGR_EVENT_DEV_DISCONNECT:
            _this.api.getCustomDevices(Convergence.getCustomDevices);
            break;
        default:
            break;
    }
},
getCustomDevices: function(aDevice) {
    var _this = Convergence;
    _this.aDevice = aDevice;

    for(var i = 0; i < aDevice.length; i++) {
        var sID = aDevice[i].getUniqueID();
        aDevice[i].registerDeviceCallback(function(oDeviceInfo) {
            _this.registerDevice(sID, oDeviceInfo);
        });
    }
},
registerDevice: function(sID, oDeviceInfo) {
    var mobileKeyEvent = jQuery.parseJSON(oDeviceInfo.data.message1);
    handleMobileEvent(mobileKeyEvent.msg);
},
sendMessage: function(oDevice, sMessage) {
    return oDevice.sendMessage(sMessage);
},
broadcastMessage: function(sMessage) {
    return this.aDevice[0] && this.aDevice[0].broadcastMessage(sMessage);
},
```

```
    uploadFile: function(sName) {
        // : image filename
        var sUrl = 'http://127.0.0.1/ws/app/' + curWidget.id  + '/file/' + sName;
        return '<img src="' + sUrl + '"/>';
    }
};
Convergence.init();



// processes the requested event
var handleMobileEvent = function(event){
    switch(event) {
        case 'msg_show' :
            $('#convergence_help').show();
            break;
        case 'msg_hide' :
            $('#convergence_help').hide();
            break;
    }
};
```

GetPath.js

```
function getAbsPath(linkString) {

    var sPath = null;
    var sLocation = window.location.href;
    var sRoot = sLocation.substring(0, sLocation.lastIndexOf('/') + 1);

    sLocation = unescape(sLocation);
    sRoot = unescape(sRoot);

    if (sRoot.indexOf('file://localhost/') != -1 && (sLocation.indexOf('C:') !=
-1 || sLocation.indexOf('D:') != -1)) {
        sPath = sRoot.split('file://localhost/')[1].replace(/\\/g, '/');
    } else if (sRoot.indexOf('file://localhost/') != -1) {
        sPath = '/' + sRoot.split('file://localhost/')[1];
```

```
    } else if (sRoot.indexOf('file://C/') != -1 || sRoot.indexOf('file://c/')
!= -1) {
        sPath = 'C://' + (sRoot.indexOf('file://C/') != -1 ? sRoot.
split('file://C/')[1] : sRoot.split('file://c/')[1]);
    } else if (sRoot.indexOf('file://D/') != -1 || sRoot.indexOf('file://d/')
!= -1) {
        sPath = 'D://' + (sRoot.indexOf('file://D/') != -1 ? sRoot.
split('file://D/')[1] : sRoot.split('file://d/')[1]);
    } else {
        sPath = sRoot;
    }


    return sPath+linkString;
}
```

Main.css

```
*
{
    padding: 0;
    margin: 0;
    border: 0;
}

/* Layout */
body
{
    width: 1280px;
    height: 720px;
    background-color: #fff;
    background : url("../../images/bg_main.jpg") no-repeat;
    overflow: hidden;
}

#scene_main{
    display: inline-block;
    width: 1280px;
```

```css
    height: 720px;
}

#header {
    height: 65px;
}

#header .slogan{
    float: left;
}

#header .appName{
    float: right;
}

#category {
    float: left;
    width: 235px;
    position: absolute;
    top: 87px;
}

#category ul{
    list-style: none;
}

#category ul li{
    width: 235px;
    height: 50px;
    color: #fff;
    font-size: 20px;
    line-height: 50px;
    text-align: center;
}

#category.focus ul li.focus{
    color: #fff;
    background: url("../../images/btn_menu.png") top;
```

```css
}

#category.focus ul li.selected{
    color: #c62ad3;
    background: url("../../images/btn_menu.png") bottom;
}

#content{
    float: right;
    position: absolute;
    left: 313px;
    top: 92px;
    width: 900px;
}

#content  > div{
    width: 100%;
    display: none;
}

#content  > div > div.title{
    display: inline-block;
    width: 380px;
    height: 23px;
}

#content.focus  > div{
    color: red;
}

#content ul {
    list-style: none;
    position: relative;
    top: 35px;
}

#content ul li{
    float: left;
```

```css
    width: 450px;
}


#content ul li img{
    width: 394px;
    height: 219px;
}


#content.focus ul li.focus img{
    border: 6px solid #c409d2;

}


#content ul li label{
    font-size: 24px;

    color: #fff;
    position: relative;
    display: block;
    top: 10px;
}


#content ul li label p{
    font-size: 18px;
    color: #acacac;
}



#scene_info{
    width: 1280px;
    height: 650px;
    background: #242424;
    position: absolute;
    top: 70px;
}

#scene_info img{
```

```css
    position: relative;
    top: 50px;
    left: 15px;
}

/*Advanced Functions*/
#header .login {
    position: absolute;
    top: 20px;
    left: 750px;
    color: #fff;
}

#header .login #login_form {
    height: 25px;
}

#header .login.focus #login_form{
    border: 6px solid #c409d2;
}

#convergence_help{
    position: absolute;
    top: 23px;
    left: 510px;
    color: #eee;
    display: none;
}

#player_container {
    position: absolute;
    width: 1280px;
    height: 720px;
    opacity: 0;
     left: 0;
     top: 0;
}
```

```css
#player_container.show {
    opacity: 1;
}
```

Praise from Samsung for
Samsung SmartTV Application Development

Written directly by the creators of the Samsung SmartTV Platform, this book provides unique insights and tips into the world of SmartTV app development. Whether you're interested in Samsung SmartTV app development for video-on-demand, gaming, multi-screen or Smart Interaction, this book includes something for everyone.

Kyungshik Lee

Service Strategy Team, Senior Vice President/Team Leader,
Visual Display Business, Samsung Electronics

This book will guide both beginners and experienced developers toward creating high-quality apps on this exciting platform. If you have any experience with web technologies, you will be able to easily start developing Samsung SmartTV applications.

Youngki Byun

S/W R&D Team, Vice President/Team Leader,
Visual Display Business, Samsung Electronics

Writers' reflection

Joonhee Ahn

Like a growing bamboo makes a new node, a growing Handstudio also makes a new node. Thank you, God! Thank you, Handstudio!

Taekyung Jeon

I learned a lot about a SmartTV application's lifecycle. The experience will aid me handsomely in future development.

Gunhee Lee

I am proud of co-authoring a book that has practical techniques and know-how of SmartTV application development.

Hyelim Cheon

I remember when I started SmartTV development. I hope that this book will help beginners, as I once was.

Hee Seo

Probably some of you have developed for mobile Android. I also transitioned from mobile apps to SmartTV convergence apps. I hope this book will help you in the transition. I especially hope this book will open new possibilities in connecting to other smart devices with the convergence feature.

Sungchan Kim

I believe that every work and thought I experienced while writing this book will hugely help me in my future growth.

Hyunghui Kim

I came to understand authors while writing this book. Thank you. I hope the information in this book will help many people.

Jiyoung Kim

I appreciate that writing this book brought me to a deeper understanding of many things that I thought I knew, but perhaps I didn't know enough.

Yeonjoo Park

Writing this book helped me greatly in reviewing many concepts. I hope this book will help all who start SmartTV development.

Yunseon Hong

I hope this book will be a lighthouse for those who are in the middle of fog.

Yoori Choi

While explaining source codes in plain language, I tried my best to grasp live ideas and intentions of the developers. It helped me with deeper understanding of information technology. I hope this book will help developers as well with planning and user experience.

Jihye Lee

I am happy for participating in recording Handstudio's years of TV app development know-how in this book.

Youngwon Lee

In the first SmartTV project three years ago, everything was solved with trial and error without a single guide book. This book might be small, but our struggles and experience will nourish SmartTV app development.

Nagyoung Kwak

For me, it was a time to reorganize our years of experience in SmartTV development. I hope this book will help all who read it.

Donghoon Kim

Extensive use of personal devices is threatening family time. But this crisis will soon be an opportunity! Your special ideas may gather families back together in the living room. Take a chance!

Mira Choi

It was a meaningful period for me to join authoring the book that has Handstudio's know-how. I hope this book helps in vitalizing the SmartTV market.

Sohyun Kim

I once received a letter from a student appealing for guidance in SmartTV programming. I hope this book will help him to become a great SmartTV developer.

Jinsoo Choi

Handstudio has grown tremendously in SmartTV programming during the last four years. I think this book helped us to stop for a while and review what we have achieved.

Seohyung Ahn

I am so proud of participating in Handstudio's first official technical book. I hope this book will provide practical help for new SmartTV application developers.

Yunghun Kang

I am grateful for the opportunity to help write this book, which is a result of Handstudio's hard work.

Special thanks to

Hyogun Lee
R&D Office Leader,
Senior Vice President
Visual Display Business,
Samsung Electronics

Kyungshik Lee
Service Strategy Team
Senior Vice President/Team Leader
Visual Display Business,
Samsung Electronics

Youngki Byun
S/W R&D Team
Vice President/Team Leader
Visual Display Business,
Samsung Electronics

Taedong Lee
Principal Engineer,
SDK Leader,
SW Platform Group,
Visual Display Business,
Samsung Electronics

Index

Index

Handstudio Co., Ltd

Handstudio is a smart TV content and service developer founded on February 1, 2010. It has developed 200 smart phone, smart pad, and smart TV applications for 153 countries. Handstudio developed Wise TV — the world's first smart TV–based contents market solution and won the first prizes of TV App Start-up Awards and Korean TV App Innovation Awards. As the world's first smart TV–contents company, Handstudio's industry-leading developers are continuously reinventing new ideas.

Website: http://www.handstudio.net
Blog: http://blog.handstudio.net
Facebook: http://facebook.com/handstudio

Tae Wook Kang

Tae Wook Kang works as a technical/legal writer for a Silicon Valley law firm and has extensively translated technical documents including Posco's automation system manual, Seoul's new traffic card system plan, iriver's mp3 player manual, and Hyundai's automobile manual. He studied International Trade at Hankuk University of Foreign Studies at Seoul, and Computer Science at San Jose State University. Before working as a translator/writer, Tae Wook founded and operated web design and programming firms Computech and Acdweb.com.

Author Handstudio Co., Ltd
Translator Tae Wook Kang
Interior Design Booknuri
Publishing Company John Wiley & Sons, Inc.
Phone 877-762-2974 or 317-572-3993
Fax 317-572-4002
Address 111 River Street, Hoboken, NJ 07030-5774
List Price $39.99
1st Edition Publishing Date 2013
ISBN 978-1-118-82802-1
Web www.wiley.com
Support www.wiley.com/techsupport